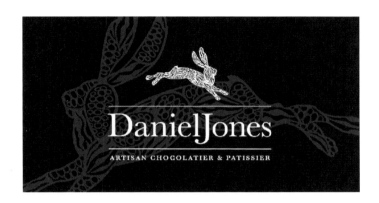

Text, recipes, photography & design
©2020 Daniel Jones

Logo designed by Harriet Parry
©2012

Edited by Rosie Griffin

First published independently in 2020 by KDP

ISBN 9798640737004

@danieljoneschoc

chocolate, infusions & magic

awards & accolades:

dedicated to Tessa and Florence

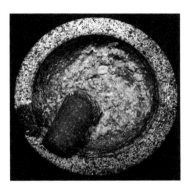

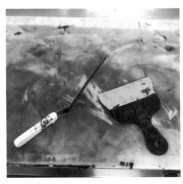

introduction

My whole life revolves around food. Wherever I travel to or take a holiday, I always have with me a fully researched list of foodie destinations to visit. I enjoy learning about the different cultures and cuisines all around the world, and love every type of food. Above all though, my absolute passion has to be chocolate.

My enthusiasm for food probably began when I was around five years old - my mum and I would bake lots of sweet treats for when my dad came home from work. He would then 'buy' some from my makeshift shop. This entrepreneurial spirit and love of cooking stayed with me throughout my childhood, and on into my college years. I trained as a chef, completing NVQs before achieving a first class honours degree in Culinary Arts Management. I met some very interesting people on my university journey, and it was during this time that my passion for chocolate and new product development was stirred.

I had discovered the magic of tempering chocolate during my university course. So the first thing I planned for after graduation was to take a trip to Paris, to eat and drink in each of the world-class patisseries, boulangeres and chocolateries there. I then continued my travels to Barbados in search of their finest sugar, and finally on to St Lucia for the ultimate experience visiting a cacao plantation.

Before and during university, I also experienced the professional kitchen environment - I started at the bottom and worked my way up, becoming a sous chef at River Cottage and then a head chef at the age of 24 at a gastro pub on the Welsh borders. I got through to the semi-finals of the prestigious 'National Chef of the Year' competition in 2011, and was also thrilled to get a mention in the Michelin guide. I loved being in the kitchen, but I was always drawn more towards the desserts section – especially the chocolate..!

My dream really was to tie together all of this experience, and open my own chocolaterie where I could sell my own handmade fresh chocolate treats. I decided to take the plunge and begin my own business, and in 2011, the brand 'Daniel Jones Artisan Chocolatier' was born. After years of planning, my dream finally came true! I imported chocolate from the Dominican Republic – this was always my preferred choice after years of tastings, plus meetings with farmers and suppliers. The chocolate itself was always fairly traded and organic. Everything was hand tempered on a marble slab in the traditional way, before being blended with unique flavour combinations.

There seemed nowhere better to set up business than the Ludlow Food Centre - Britain's best food hall, and luckily local to me. I will never forget the day that I pitched my business venture to them in order to secure the rental of a manufacturing kitchen. I organised my business plan, made a silky smooth batch of my water ganache, and presented it to owner Reuben Crouch. Little did I know then that the pitch and those truffles would open up so many doors for me, and allow my chocolate dreams to come true - as well as giving me an amazing new friendship with Reuben.

My creative mind was able to run free in this new space, and I soon had a full range of filled, bar and drinking chocolates. I was grateful to win various awards, including the prestigious 'Great Taste' accolade for my tonka bean bar and passion fruit caramels. I also won Theo Paphitis' 'Small Business Sunday' (#SBS) award.

I had hundreds of stockists around the United Kingdom and Europe, and my online shop enabled me to also ship globally. I toured the country to attend food festivals and spread the love for real chocolate. I absolutely loved this time working with chocolate every day, but running your own business is extremely hard work. I eventually decided to close my business - after three years - during this period, I had realised all of my dreams and more. I continued to channel my creativity into the Ludlow Food Centre though, becoming their new product development and production manager.

Here I managed eight different professional kitchen spaces, including preserves, butchery, packaging and more – as well managing the 140 cover restaurant, 15 bedroom hotel and the high street deli. It was also my job to create and oversee exciting new product lines and innovative concepts. I did this for a very fulfilling two years, before a new opportunity came knocking at my door…!

This was an offer from a company called 'Blue Sky Botanics' to work for them creating botanical extracts, infusions and distillates for the food and drink industry - an offer I couldn't refuse! My creativity can again run wild here, and I've even managed to return of course to my first passion, by extracting every part of the fantastic cacao fruit! After being in this new role for four years, I won the prestigious award for 'Top New Talent' from the Grocer magazine in 2019.

I still do the occasional chocolate demonstration, travelling with the amazing 'Wot's Cooking' team - whose founders Glyn and Katie have always supported me on my journey. I still love teaching people about chocolate and how romantic and versatile this fruit really is. Whenever I do a demonstration, I always get asked where my recipes can be found - and so this has been the main inspiration for me to write this book.

I will now take you on a magical chocolate journey where we will look at the history of this amazing fruit, before understanding the differences between the main varieties. We will then look at the basic tempering techniques, and use these to create stunning bars, truffles, drinks and even some savoury meals.

I hope you have a choc-tastic time!

Daniel x

where it all began

Chocolate is made from the fruit of the cacao tree, native to Central and South America. The fruit from the trees are called pods, and each pod contains around forty beans. The story of cacao farming began around 1500 BC. The indigenous cultures developing at this time in parts of Mexico and Central America were the first to grow the trees as a domestic crop. These people were the Mesoamericans, and they called the trees 'kakaw'. One such tribe - the Olmecs - are thought to have been the first to use the brightly coloured pods, by cracking them open to create a ceremonial drink. As they kept no written history, it is unclear whether they used the beans in these drinks, or just the pulp of the pod.

The Olmecs certainly passed their knowledge onto the Mayans - another famous Mesoamerican civilisation. The Mayans were the first to really experience chocolate, and they worshipped it. They fermented and ground the beans, before adding chilli and other local spices. They named this drink 'xocolatl' or 'kuku-u-kul' which translates as 'bitter water', and they drank it at important ceremonial rituals. Even though it was very important in Mayan culture, the drink wasn't just kept for the wealthy and powerful – it was available for almost everyone to enjoy with their meals.

The next ancient civilisation of chocolate enthusiasts was the Aztecs, who conquered the Mayans. The Aztecs continued the Mayan belief that the trees were given to them by their gods, and they also enjoyed the spiced beverages which they called 'chcahuatl'- which some think is where the modern word chocolate comes from. Others think chocolate comes from another Aztec word 'choqui', which means warmth. Both the Mayans and the Aztecs also used the beans as an early form of currency, and they were considered more valuable than gold.

Many hundreds of years later, chocolate made its way across to Europe. During the 16th century, explorers Christopher Columbus and Hernán Cortés travelled to South America to establish Spanish colonies. They were greeted by the Aztecs in the courts of the emperor Montezuma, who served the explorers his favourite spicy drink. They promptly took some home with them to Spain, and first used the word 'cacao', as the Spanish interpretation of the original 'kakaw'. The drink was taken as a medicine first of all, until the Spanish developed the bitter taste into a more delicious recipe by sweetening it with sugar, vanilla, nutmeg and other warm spices. The drink became fashionable at the Spanish king's court where it was kept secret for almost 100 years.

It finally began to grow in popularity throughout Europe during the 17th century, and was 'the' drink of the aristocracies. It's thought that when English traders brought the beans home, they actually misspelled the Spanish 'cacao', and so the name 'cocoa' was born here in the United Kingdom. London's first 'chocolate house' was opened in 1657 by a Frenchman, beginning the hot chocolate drink craze. By the 1700s, there were chocolate houses on many street corners across the whole of Europe. It became so popular that in 1753, the Swedish botanist Carl Linnaeus (who classified plants and animals with Latin names) chose *theobroma cacao* for the cacao tree – meaning 'food of the gods'.

Up until this point, chocolate had only ever been consumed as a drink. But this started to change in the late 18th century, when the race began to create chocolate products for the masses. During this period, the English city of Bristol was a major port where ships travelled to and from the 'New World' of the America's, bringing cocoa in plentiful supply. A man called Joseph Fry began to sell cocoa from his Bristol shop in around 1756. He was a Quaker and stood against alcohol, so he saw chocolate as a nutritious alternative. In 1761 he acquired a patent with his partner John Vaughan for a water-powered machine that could grind cocoa flakes into powder to produce a better drink. After Joseph's death, the business was taken over by his wife and son (J.S. Fry), who tweaked the process –by installing one of James Watt's steam engines at the Bristol chocolate works, and revolutionising cocoa powder production in Britain.

European manufacturers were quick to follow suit. In Holland during 1828, father and son team Casparus and Coenraad van Houten invented both a hydraulic cocoa press (which could separate the fat from a cacao bean, leaving a more refined powder), and the 'Dutching' process of treating chocolate with an alkali for a milder and smoother taste. The finer powder was much nicer to enjoy as a drink, and people started adding milk to it instead of water. This also meant that cocoa could be mass-produced, which made it cheaper and readily available to the wider European public.

Back in Bristol, J.S. Fry had made his sons partners in their business and J.S. Fry and Sons was born. In the 1820s, Fry and Sons were using forty per cent of the cocoa imported into Britain. Their greatest innovation came when they mixed cocoa powder with sugar and cocoa fat, creating a paste that could then be moulded into a bar. This was in 1847, and so the very first chocolate bar was born - changing chocolate from just a drink into a popular snack for the masses. Fry and Sons sold this new product under the French name 'chocolat delicieux a manger' (which translates as 'delicious chocolate to eat'), and it resembled the dark chocolate of today.

Swiss chocolatier Daniel Peter created the first lighter milk chocolate drink product in Europe in 1857, by adding powdered milk to the cocoa mix. Peter lived in the town of Vevey, and had another innovative neighbour, in the form of confectioner Henri Nestlé. These two men combined their talents, with Nestlé supplying condensed milk to Peter from 1875, helping him to develop the first milk chocolate bar. In 1904, Nestlé began selling chocolate for the first time in Europe when it took over export sales from Peter's company. At the same time, another famous Swiss chocolatier called Rudolphe Lindt invented a process that agitated and stirred chocolate for hours. This was known as 'conching', and it created a super smooth and creamy chocolate with an outstanding aroma and excellent melting characteristics.

But it was the Bristolian Fry and Sons who had taken the prize for creating that very first bar of chocolate, and they were also responsible for the first chocolate egg in 1873. Decorating eggs at Easter time had been a popular Christian tradition for centuries, and Fry decided to create a chocolate version. However, in 1919, Fry and Sons merged with another British company more famous these days for making chocolate Easter eggs – Cadbury's.

John Cadbury was another Quaker with the same values as Fry - in 1824, he similarly began his business career selling alternatives to alcohol from his shop in Birmingham. He became a manufacturer too, joining with his brother and sons to open a factory. While they were not as fast to develop a chocolate bar, Cadbury's launched many new products themselves during the late 1800's. During this period, they also built their 'factory in a garden' in Bournville, four miles outside of Birmingham, to provide a clean and healthy working environment for employees. Fry and Sons were not innovators like Cadbury's, and the conditions at Bourneville were much better than Fry's factory in Bristol. The city-centre location of Fry's was also unsuitable for bringing in fresh milk, and they were using dried milk powder as a substitute. In contrast, Cadbury's were investing in modern technology like their own cocoa-press in 1866, and creating new products with fresh ingredients - such as their famous 'Dairy Milk' in 1905. J.S. Fry & Sons decided to cut their losses, and merged with Cadbury's in 1919. By 1930, Cadbury was the 24th-largest British manufacturing company, and went on to take direct control of the under-performing Fry and Sons factory five years later.

It wasn't long before America also acquired a taste for modern chocolate, as the products and innovations filtered over from Europe. The man who started it all across the pond was Milton S. Hershey. He was born in 1857, and took an apprenticeship with a candy maker after leaving school, before founding his hugely successful 'Caramel Company' in 1883. Ten years later, he visited the World's Columbian Exposition held in Chicago (the first 'world's fair') and became fascinated with the exhibit of German chocolate-making machinery. He bought the equipment for his factory and soon began producing a variety of chocolate products. Through trial and error, Hershey developed his own formula for solid milk chocolate to sell to the American public, and in 1905 he completed construction of what was to become the world's largest chocolate manufacturing plant, using the latest mass production techniques. Hershey's milk chocolate quickly became the first marketed product of its kind in the United States, and the company is still America's favourite chocolate maker to this day.

With so many innovations evolving across the world, the late 19th and early 20th centuries were a period of major advancement in the global chocolate industry. The popularity of chocolate products has soared ever since, with consumption reaching its peak between the end of World War II and the 1980's, and it has never declined. The global chocolate market was estimated to be worth $131.7 billion in 2019 - quite different from days of the Aztec tribes when 1 rabbit would have cost you just 10 kakaw beans...

from tree to bar

Growing

Theobroma cacao grows approximately twenty degrees either side of the equator, in what is sometimes known as the 'chocolate band'. This is a warm temperature range across the equator where cacao pods can grow.

Climate	25-27°C
Rainfall	1250-2500mm/year
Growing Conditions	under shade canopies
Soil	well drained, fertile and slightly acidic
Height	12-15mtr
Pod size	15-35cm in length
Pod contains	20-75 beans
Nutrients	Beans = 50% cocoa butter (fat); 25% carbohydrate; 25% protein, theobromine, vitamins and minerals

Varieties

There are more than ten different varieties of cacao, but they are each generally considered to be in one of three main categories: Forastero, Trinitario and Criollo.

Forastero cacaos are native to the Amazon region, and account for more than 80% of the world's cacao. Today, it is grown in Ecuador, Brazil and as far afield as Africa and South East Asia, and it produces a fantastic, high yielding crop. It has a very dark and robust flavour profile, and the beans are red and purple in colour. Forastero is mainly used for bulk or mass produced chocolate, although there are exceptions. For example, the sub-type Nacional is the oldest and rarest cacao variety in the world, dating back at least 5,300 years in Ecuador and as recently as 2009, pure Nacional cacao was believed to be extinct. However one of the last surviving groves of 100% pure Nacional cacao has been since found, and is considered one of the finest varieties in the world. Examples of other Forastero sub-types are Amelonado, Cundeamor and Calabacillo and each offers slightly different cocoa tastes, with Amelonado being the most widely cultivated.

Criollo beans are grown in Central and South America, the Caribbean, the Philippines and Sri Lanka. It is the oldest known cacao variety, and now only accounts for less than ten percent of our cocoa supply. The beans have an incredible depth of aroma and a complex flavour profile, and some of the Venezualan sub-types include Chuao, Porcelana and Puerto Cabello. Criollo beans are delicately pink and white in colour, and produce a lower yield than other varieties. Sadly they are also more vulnerable to disease and environmental threats, which all contributes to making them the rarest type of beans. In my opinion, they are the finest in the world and make the most extraordinary bar of chocolate!

Trinitario is a hybrid of Criollo and Forastero varieties, and originated on the island of Trinidad. The beans are complex and aromatic, and take some of the best traits from the other two types. They have the flavours from Criollo and the hardiness, high yields and disease resistance from Forastero. Trinitario varieties were actually created by accident, after a Trinidadian hurricane or cacao disease destroyed all existing Criollo trees in the 1720s. The local farmers then decided to replant with Forastero varieties, but cross-pollination must have occurred with surviving Criollo trees, and the new cacao beans began to grow. Trinitario cocoa is now grown throughout the world in Venezuala, Ecuador, Madagascar, Sri Lanka, Cameroon, and parts of South East Asia, but still only makes up five percent of the total world production.

The process

Fermenting
This is the first and most critical stage of the chocolate making process. Cacao beans are fermented either in wooden boxes or on the ground under banana leaves. The cacao pulp surrounding the bean naturally breaks down and begins the process of flavour development.

Drying
After fermentation, the beans are dried – either naturally out in the sun, or laid on hot mats or flooring. This part of the process is important to ensure the beans are microbiologically safe and can then be stored for up to five years even after exportation.

Roasting
In order to enhance the flavour profile, the beans are roasted at different temperatures and humidity levels and for varying lengths of time, depending on the bean and the chocolate requirements.

Winnowing
Once the beans have been perfectly roasted, they are winnowed, which removes the outer husk. These are a waste product of the chocolate making process, although they still have lots of flavour and are perfect for an infusion!

Grinding
The beans are then ground between rollers to create a chocolate paste, known as chocolate liquor. At this stage, the liquor can be separated into two – cocoa mass (or powder) and cocoa butter (the fat). You can try the grinding process yourself at home, using a slightly warm pestle and mortar to grind down some cacao nibs. They will eventually turn into liquid, although it may take a long time to get them completely smooth. If you set this in a mould, it would create a 100 percent cocoa chocolate bar.

Theobroma,

**the cacao genus name,
is taken from the Greek for**

"food of the gods"

Conching

To make silky smooth chocolate, conching must occur. This is a process where a certain amount of cocoa mass and cocoa butter are mixed together with other ingredients such as sugar or milk, and then slowly combined until refined. This process can take between twenty four hours and two weeks. Conching ensures that all ingredients are well mixed, which creates a velvety smooth consistency. It also reduces acidity and allows for exquisite, well balanced and complex flavours to be developed. This is the stage where you alter the cocoa percentage of your chocolate, and make either darker or lighter products.

Tempering

This is the key stage in giving the finished chocolate product a perfect, shiny surface and a clean, crisp snap. Within cocoa butter, there are several different types of fat molecules – all of which melt at different temperatures. If chocolate was melted with an uncontrolled temperature then different sizes crystals would form. This causes a matte white finish and a crumbly texture once set. In order to make crystals of equal size and end up with a higher quality product, then the chocolate must be tempered. This is where chocolate is heated, cooled and then heated again.

To read more about the tempering process, see page 19.

Moulding

The final stage is to pour the liquid tempered chocolate into a mould and allow it to set. The resulting solid bar of chocolate will generally have a shelf life of up to two years before the flavour and aroma begin to deteriorate.

Tasting

Taste = senses on our tongue

Aroma = senses in our nose

Flavour = where taste meets aroma

Eating or tasting chocolate should be a complete and exciting full sensory experience. Chocolate is a very complex product with over four hundred different flavour compounds. Each stage of the process described previously has a major impact on the taste of the finished chocolate product.

Personally I like a piece of chocolate in the evening, although I would always recommend trying chocolate at different times of day. Chocolate eaten in the morning will taste different to the evening - when you wake up, your body has gone several hours without any food and you will naturally have a higher sensitivity to the taste of sugar, salt and protein at any time when you need to eat.

Tasting tips

i.   **Look** at the chocolate. Is it shiny? Does it appear smooth?

ii.   Break the chocolate between your fingers, and **hear** the snap!

iii.   **Touch** the chocolate, rub it between your fingers, and feel for a silky smooth texture.

iv.   Release the aroma and inhale the **smell**!

v.   Place the chocolate on your tongue and allow your body temperature to naturally melt it, releasing all of the delicate flavour profiles and **tastes.**

vi.   Once melted, swallow the chocolate and inhale the deep overall flavour.

vii.   Finally, enjoy the 'finish'. Chocolate has lingering notes which can last for up to ten minutes on the palate.

If tasting multiple chocolates in one sitting, have a palate cleanser to hand (water biscuits to clean the palette and then actual water to wash all contaminants away). It's also best to start with chocolate with a lower percentage of cocoa, and work your way up.

Flavour profiles

Each cacao variety can grow in most of the countries in the 'chocolate band', but here are the general flavour profiles for specific areas:

Caribbean – fruity, floral - extremely complex *(Criollo and Trinitario)*

South America – fruity, earthy, burnt wood, tannin *(Trinitario and Nacional)*

Africa – nutty, spicy, wood, tobacco, smoke *(Forastero)*

Madagascar – citrus, oily, green *(Criollo and Trinitario)*

India – creamy, toffee, fruity *(Criollo and Trinitario)*

South East Asia – vanilla, caramel, toffee, treacle, red berry, woody, spicy – very complex *(Criollo and Trinitario)*

ganache

A ganache is basically an emulsification of chocolate and a liquid (traditionally cream). It was first thought to have been created at the Pâtisserie Siraudin in Paris in 1850, when an apprentice pâtissier spilled cream into a bowl of melted chocolate. This velvety smooth and silky mix now forms the base of truffles, spreads and glazes worldwide.

I do love the traditional French ganache which uses cream, but I personally find that sometimes dairy can mask the flavour of the chocolate - particularly if I am also incorporating delicate flavours into chocolate truffles through the use of infusions.

We know that a ganache is an emulsification of a fat (always chocolate for a ganache) and a liquid. This can be anything you want, such as cream, milk, infused or plain water, fruit juice or puree, alcohol - the possibilities are endless!

The classic ganache uses equal quantities of chocolate and cream. Once you have mastered it, you can experiment with different flavours and textures. If you want a firmer ganache for truffles, you can increase the chocolate content. If you want a softer ganache - maybe for icing a cake - then you can simply increase the amount of liquid.

The classic ganache

200g chocolate (55%)
200g double cream

i.   Place the chocolate into a heatproof bowl.

ii. Heat the cream in a saucepan until just simmering. Do not allow to boil.

iii. Rest the cream for 2-3 minutes. If you do not rest the cream and pour hot liquid directly onto the chocolate, there is a risk it will split or burn.

iv. Pour the rested warm cream over the chocolate and mix thoroughly with a spoonula. It may look as if it is starting to split, but this is the fat trying to mix with the liquid, like trying to mix oil with water. All you need to do is persevere and mix well.

v.   Allow the mixture to cool at room temperature, and then chill until required.

tempering

As mentioned previously, a perfect bar of chocolate will have a glossy, high shine and a clean 'snap' when broken. This is the sign of a well-tempered chocolate.

There are actually six different types of fat molecules in chocolate, which all melt at different temperatures. This makes the chocolate very unstable, visually unpleasant and gives it a crumbly texture. To overcome this, we can 'temper' or pre-crystallise the chocolate.

Scientifically, tempering is the process of bringing chocolate to its correct crystalline form. This is done by controlling the amount of time it is heated for, the temperature itself and how much the chocolate is moved around. The chocolate should be melted at between 45-49°C; then cooled to 27-28°C; then reheated back up to 29°C for white/ruby chocolate, 30°C for milk chocolate, or 31°C for dark chocolate. This is known as the 'working temperature'.

Melting your chocolate

To achieve the best flavour profile for your chocolate, it is best to melt it slowly for a longer time, rather than quickly over boiling water. This will make sure that the different fat molecules have all melted at their correct temperatures.

i.   Bring a pan of water to the boil.

ii.   Remove from the heat and place the bowl of chocolate on top.

iii.   Allow the steam to slowly melt the chocolate, and stir from time to time.

iv.   Do not allow your chocolate to exceed 49°C.

Depending on how much chocolate you are melting, you may need to remove the bowl and return the pan to the heat to create more steam. Make sure you do not get any liquid or condensation into your chocolate, as it will ruin the chocolate and make it impossible to temper. Generally speaking, you can melt about one kilogram of chocolate in about one hour using the steam produced from the first water boil.

Once you have melted your chocolate, there are two tempering methods to choose from - the traditional 'marble slab' way, or the 'seeding' method.

The marble slab method

i. Take two-thirds of your melted chocolate and pour directly onto your marble slab. Using a spatula and a scraper, carefully move the chocolate around. This will cool and thicken the chocolate. Aim for 27-28°C.

ii. Once cooled, scrape the chocolate into the remaining one-third of still warm chocolate. This should increase the chocolate to the appropriate 'working temperature' depending on your type of chocolate.

The seeding method

i. Weigh 500g of melted chocolate into one bowl.

ii. Weigh 250g of solid chocolate pieces into a second bowl.

iii. Slowly add a handful at a time of the solid pieces to the melted chocolate. Stir vigorously and repeat until all the chocolate pieces are used and are melted. The aim here is to cool the chocolate to 27-28°C, and again the chocolate will thicken as it cools.

iv. Very carefully, heat the chocolate back up to the correct 'working temperature'. The best way to do this is through small blasts of heat, using a hairdryer. Heat and stir but be careful not to overheat.

Checking your temper

The best way to check your temper is by using a temperature probe. If you don't have one, you can dip a palette knife into the chocolate and touch your bottom lip. It should feel the same as your body temperature – not too warm and not too cool! You can also check by dipping the tip of the knife into the chocolate, removing and leaving it in a cool place. If the chocolate is tempered correctly, it should set within minutes and look glossy.

Basic chocolate rules and tips

Once you have mastered both a ganache and a tempering technique, you can create anything you want out of chocolate! Remember - when tempering, do NOT add any liquid, and do NOT store in the fridge. When making a ganache, DO add liquid and DO store in the fridge!

If you have any leftover tempered chocolate, spread it out flat on a flexible baking mat to cool. You can then break it up and keep in a sealed jar, to be re-melted for your next batch of tempered chocolate or to be used in hot chocolates or a ganache. I always have a jar of chocolate bits in my kitchen! The perfect temperature in your kitchen for chocolate work is 18-20°C, and the perfect working humidity is 50%.

1
melt

2
cool

tempering
step-by-step

My House Collection from Daniel Jones Artisan Chocolatier.

DanielJones
ARTISAN CHOCOLATIER & PATISSIER

HOUSE BLEND
MOCHA
A 'real' mocha mix made with
stunning Dominican Republic
chocolate. Simply add milk for a
perfect cup of mocha at home! Our
toasty and intense house blend gives
you the perfect balance of chocolate
and coffee, with strong bitter
caramel notes.

125g e

DanielJones
ARTISAN CHOCOLATIER & PATISSIER

HOUSE BLEND
MILK
HOT CHOCOLATE
A 'real' hot chocolate mix made
with stunning Dominican Republic
37% chocolate. Simply add milk
for a perfect cup of hot chocolate
at home! Our milk blend results
in a very creamy drink, with sweet
caramel notes.

125g e

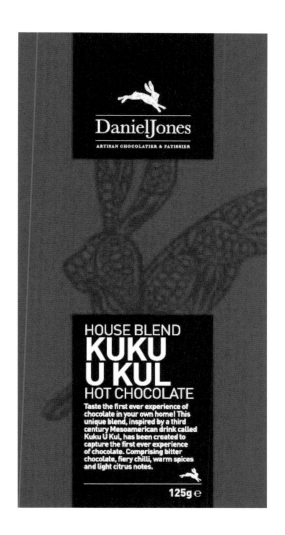

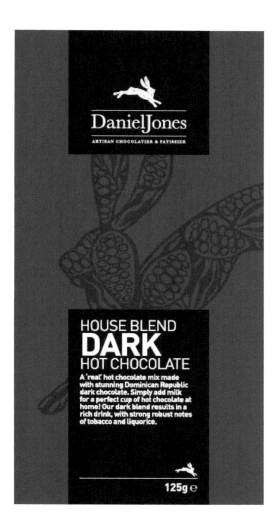

My Drinks Collection from Daniel Jones Artisan Chocolatier.

Daniel Jones
ARTISAN CHOCOLATIER & PATISSIER

COOKIES
& CREAM

A creamy milk bar, decorated with white chocolate and textures of cookie

60g ℮

Daniel Jones
ARTISAN CHOCOLATIER & PATISSIER

FRUIT
& NUT

A 55% bar with stunning natural fruit flavours, studded with flame raisins, cherries, apricots & hazelnuts

60g ℮

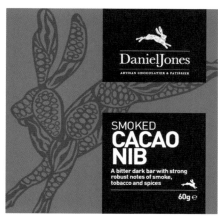

Daniel Jones
ARTISAN CHOCOLATIER & PATISSIER

SMOKED
**CACAO
NIB**

A bitter dark bar with strong robust notes of smoke, tobacco and spices

60g ℮

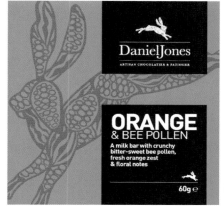

Daniel Jones
ARTISAN CHOCOLATIER & PATISSIER

ORANGE
& BEE POLLEN

A milk bar with crunchy bitter-sweet bee pollen, fresh orange zest & floral notes

60g ℮

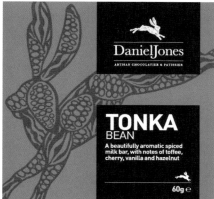

Daniel Jones
ARTISAN CHOCOLATIER & PATISSIER

TONKA
BEAN

A beautifully aromatic spiced milk bar, with notes of toffee, cherry, vanilla and hazelnut

60g ℮

Daniel Jones
ARTISAN CHOCOLATIER & PATISSIER

FRESH
MINT
CRUNCH

A naturally fruity 55% bar infused with fresh mint, caramelised chocolate & Barbados amber sugar

60g ℮

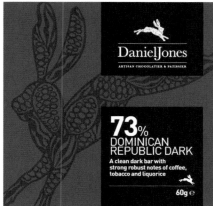

Daniel Jones
ARTISAN CHOCOLATIER & PATISSIER

73%
DOMINICAN
REPUBLIC DARK

A clean dark bar with strong robust notes of coffee, tobacco and liquorice

60g ℮

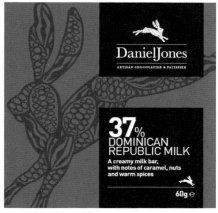

Daniel Jones
ARTISAN CHOCOLATIER & PATISSIER

37%
DOMINICAN
REPUBLIC MILK

A creamy milk bar, with notes of caramel, nuts and warm spices

60g ℮

Daniel Jones
ARTISAN CHOCOLATIER & PATISSIER

DOMINICAN
REPUBLIC
WHITE

An extra creamy 'real' white chocolate bar with notes of vanilla, butterscotch and toffee

60g ℮

Daniel Jones
ARTISAN CHOCOLATIER & PATISSIER

FESTIVE
SPICE

A dark 73% chocolate bar, infused with allspice, cassia, orange & nutmeg

60g ℮

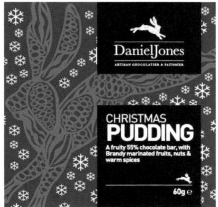

Daniel Jones
ARTISAN CHOCOLATIER & PATISSIER

CHRISTMAS
PUDDING

A fruity 55% chocolate bar, with Brandy marinated fruits, nuts & warm spices

60g ℮

Daniel Jones
ARTISAN CHOCOLATIER & PATISSIER

GINGERBREAD
CRUNCH

A 'real' white chocolate bar with textures of spiced gingerbread and a hint of vanilla

60g ℮

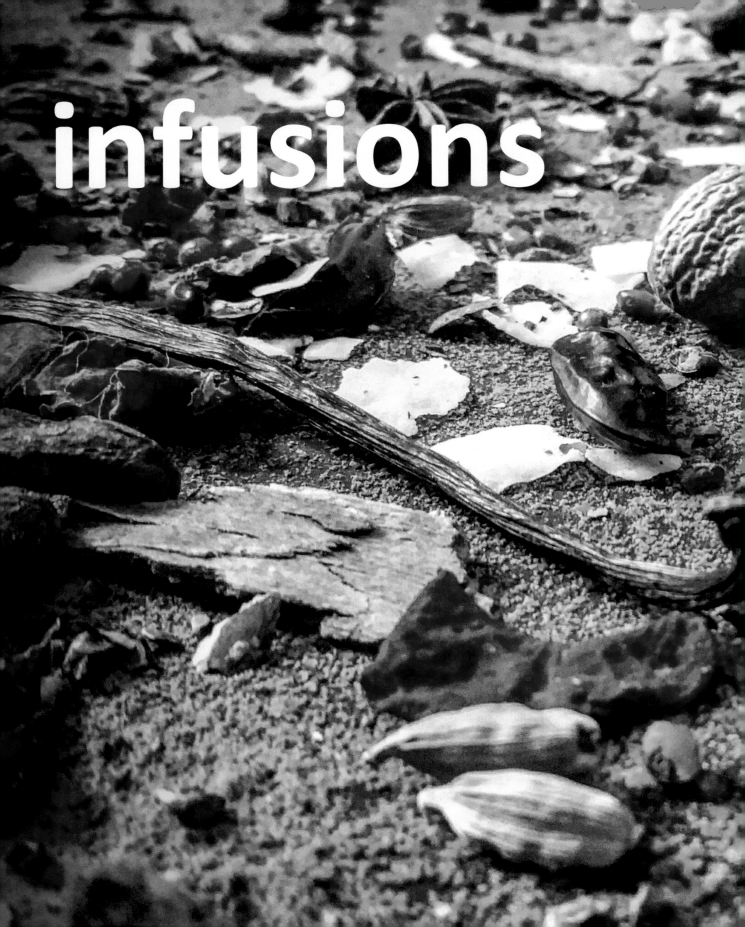

infusions

infusions

An infusion is the process of extracting compounds from a botanical, using a solvent such as water, oil, sugar or ethanol. That sounds very scientific, but simply it is where flavour wizardry happens!

It is like making a cup of tea - you pop your teabag into hot water, and leave to brew. The result is an infusion of a classic cuppa, where the botanical is the tea, the solvent is the water, and you have used temperature and time to create it.

Botanical
any part of a plant, including edible herbs, spices, flowers, fruits, roots, barks, seeds, or leaves.

Solvent
any suitable liquid, including water, oil, alcohol, sugar syrup, glycerine, fruit juice, cream, etc.

Temperature
depending on the botanical, you can heat to anywhere between 5-100°C. Generally, the hotter the liquid, the more bitter and astringent notes you can extract. To make things more complicated though, every botanical is unique and different!

Time
again, this depends but can be anywhere between 3 minutes to 12 months or more. Generally speaking, you can make a really good infusion in 24 hours, but some botanicals such as roots and spices need longer to work their magic, with the optimum time being around 7 days. A long infusion would be for a product like sloe gin, where the fruits can steep in alcohol for up to a year.

Try an infusion for yourself! Take some fresh coriander, and infuse in water for 3 hours, 24 hours and 7 days. Taste the difference - you will be amazed!

However, there does come a point where the solvent will reach saturation point, where it won't take on anymore flavour from the botanical - regardless of how much longer you leave it. You will only discover this through trial and error, but I have developed a few recipes for you to try which are great to keep in your cupboards at home. Personally I like to use infusions to delicately flavour a ganache, or to add different layers and top notes to a drink.

elderflower & meadowsweet syrup

Makes approx. 800g

I love foraging. One of the most beautiful aromas in the air during early summer is elderflower. Our native plant grows in hedgerows across Britain, but there are actually over 160 varieties, each with their own distinctive flavour, aroma and colour! So try this simple recipe with any varieties you can find and taste the difference between them! (p.s. My favourite white elder variety is "Florence")

775g sugar
225g water
1/8 tsp citric acid
150g fresh elderflower
25g fresh meadowsweet

i. Heat the sugar, water and citric acid until the sugar is fully dissolved. Allow to fully cool.

ii. Add the freshly picked elderflowers and meadowsweet to the cooled syrup. Allow to infuse for 24 hours.

iii. Drain the liquor through a piece of muslin cloth, discarding the flowers.

Storage:
Use immediately in a ganache, drink or ice cream.
Refrigerate and use within 1 month.
Pasteurise* and use within 3 months.
Freeze and use within 1 year.

* How to pasteurise:

i. Heat the syrup in a pan to 80°C and hold for 10 minutes. Pour into sterilised bottles or jars and seal immediately.

ii. Allow to cool at room temperature.

iii. Label and store in a fridge.

oleo citri saccharum

Makes approx. 125g

This is the secret ingredient in any cocktail mixologists bar! The Latin name translates to mean 'oily sugar'. All you need is citrus peel, sugar and a little time to pack an incredible punch! The sugar draws out all of the incredibly aromatic essential oils.

50g lemon peel
50g orange peel
sprig of rose geranium
sprig of anise hyssop
200g cane sugar

i. Place the peel, and herbs in a bowls. Cover with sugar.

ii. Leave for 24-48 hours and watch the magic happen!

iii. Drain the mixture through a piece of muslin cloth and press well. You will be left with a delicious citrus syrup. Store in the

There are hundreds of artisan gins now being made in small craft distilleries around the UK. Here is my take on this incredibly complex botanical drink!

If you have a copper still, you can distil the botanicals yourself, if not, you can simply infuse them (this will make a dark brown gin, but still with an amazing flavour!)

50g juniper berries
20g coriander seed
15g angelica root
10g cassia bark
25g fresh lemongrass
20g blood orange peel
20g fresh verbena
5g black peppercorn
2g cardamom
5g liquorice
30g cacao nibs
360g water
95g plain vodka

There are two methods of making this - one is to extract the botanicals in a liquor, the second is to steam distil them.

Infusing

i. Place all of the botanicals in a glass jar.

ii. Cover with the water and vodka. Seal with a lid and give it a good shake.

iii. Leave at ambient temperature for approximately 7 days. You can leave for as long as you want, but I have found 7 days is the perfect amount of time to extract all of the warm spice notes balanced with the sweet citrus.

iv. Drain through two pieces of muslin cloth and return to a clean, sterilised jar. Use as required, or store at ambient temperature for up to 12 months.

Distilling

i. To distil professionally you need an alembic still. But there is a way to do this yourself at home with a steamer and some ice!

ii. Half fill a saucepan with cold water. Insert a steamer basket and rest a bowl on top (to catch the aromatic water).

iii. Spread the dry and fresh botanicals around the bowl directly onto the steamer basket.

iv. Invert the lid of the pan so that it sits upside down. Place a heaped amount of ice onto the top of the lid.

v. Turn on the heat to low and simmer very gently for about 1-2 hours. Do not allow to boil or the pan to dry out.

vi. During the distillation, the warm water will rise, passing through the spices, before hitting the lid of the pan. The ice will help to cool the water down, creating condensation. This will then slowly drip down into the bowl, leaving behind an aromatic water, similar to that of gin!

vii. After about 2 hours, turn off the heat and set aside for one hour. Once cooled, remove the lid and carefully lift out the bowl.

viii. Once cool, add the ethanol. For every 60g of water, add 40g of vodka. Mix well and pour into a clean, sterilised bottle. Store for up to 12 months at ambient temperature. Use as you would vanilla extract.

masala chai infusion

Makes approx. 300g

You can pretty much extract or infuse any botanical - the photo opposite shows just a few! This recipe is inspired from a drink that I had whilst travelling through the magical country of India.

30g Darjeeling tea	i. Place all of the spices in a glass jar.
20g cardamom	
30g cinnamon	ii. Cover with the water and vodka. Seal with a lid and give it a good shake.
15g nutmeg	
65g cassia	iii. Leave at ambient temperature for approximately 5 days. You can leave for as long as you want, but I have found 5 days is the perfect amount of time to extract all of the warm spice notes balanced with the sweet vanilla.
5g vanilla	
10g turmeric	
30g cacao nib	
360g water	
95g plain vodka	iv. Drain through two pieces of muslin cloth and return to a clean, sterilised jar. Use as required, or store at ambient temperature for up to 6 months. Use as you would vanilla extract.

From top left; liquorice root, black tea, cinnamon, saffron, dried mint, smoked paprika, lime flower, sesame seed, coriander seed, cacao husk, juniper berries, cocoa butter, cloves, dried meadowsweet, vanilla pod, nutmeg, rose petals, tonka beans, cacao nibs, matcha tea, star anise, turmeric, cardamom pods, pink peppercorns, cascara, fennel seed, cassia, Himalayan sea salt, coconut, black cardamom

rose limoncello

Makes approx. 900g

The most incredible aromatic lemons come from Amalfi in Italy. Limoncello is a traditional Italian liquor and paired with beautifully scented floral roses - well, it is a match made in heaven!

10 lemons (150g zest)
225g plain vodka
525g water
10 edible fresh rose heads
250g water
400g cane sugar

i. Infuse the zest in the vodka and water for 1 month. Store in either a stainless steel or glass container

ii. Add the rose petals and infuse for a further 3 days.

iii. Make the syrup by heating the sugar and the smaller amount of water in a pan until dissolved. Allow to fully cool.

iv. Meanwhile, drain the lemon mixture through a piece of muslin cloth, discarding the lemon peel and geranium. Mix the drained liquor with the cool syrup. Pour into sterilised bottles and mature for at least 2 weeks. The longer you leave it, the better it becomes! Drink over ice or use as required.

mulled wine liqueur

Makes approx. 500g

Inspired by my favourite time of the year, Christmas. Walking through the festive street markets, wrapped up in your woolly hat and gloves, with the wonderful aroma of warming, aromatic spices ... it's a traditional Christmas atmosphere!

50g haskap berries
50g elderberries
10g allspice
25g cinnamon
20g star anise
45g orange zest
15g vanilla
640g water
170g plain vodka

i.   Place the fruit and spices in a glass jar.

ii.   Cover with the water and vodka. Seal with a lid and give it a good shake.

iii.   Leave at ambient temperature for approximately 4 weeks. You can leave for as long as you want, the longer you leave it the stronger and more complex the flavours will become.

iv.   Drain through two pieces of muslin cloth and return to a clean, sterilised jar. Use as required, or store at ambient temperature for up to 12 months. Use as you would vanilla extract or drink.

bars

award-winning tonka bean

Makes approx. 6 x 60g bars

One of my absolute favourite spices! It is native to Brazil, South America and is highly aromatic, with notes of cherries, hazelnut and vanilla. It is extremely potent and one tiny bean is enough to flavour about 100 chocolate bars! I was thrilled to win a Gold with this recipe in the 2012 Great Taste Awards.

400g milk chocolate (I would recommend 36% Dominican Republic for this one!)

1 tonka bean

i. Temper the chocolate (*see page 19*)

ii. Finely grate in the tonka bean and thoroughly stir. Pour into a polished mould and lightly grate a tiny amount of tonka bean on top of each bar.

iii. Allow to set at room temperature for 24 hours.

iv. The following day, demould by bending and banging the mould on the work surface. If tempered correctly they should fall straight out and have a shiny surface.

v. Wrap in paper or plastic bags. Store at ambient temperature for up

cookies & cream

Makes approx. 6 x 60g bars

This is really inspired by drinking a glass of milk as a child, always having a stack of chocolate chip cookies to dunk in and savouring every moment!

400g 37% milk chocolate
100g white chocolate

6 of your favourite cookies

i. Temper the milk chocolate (*see page 19*). Set aside.

ii. Temper the white chocolate (*see page 19*). Set aside.

iii. Pour into a polished mould. Sprinkle the crushed cookies on top and finish with a swirl of white chocolate.

iv. Allow to set at room temperature for 24 hours.

v. The following day, demould by bending and banging the mould on the work surface. If tempered correctly they should fall straight out and have a shiny surface.

vi. Wrap in paper or plastic bags. Store at ambient

mint chocolate crunch

Makes approx. 6 x 60g bars

350g 55% chocolate
1tbsp fresh mint
30g chocolate crunch*

i. Temper the chocolate (*see page 19*)

ii. Add the chopped mint and chocolate crunch (reserve 1tbsp of chocolate crunch for decoration) to the chocolate. Pour into a polished mould and sprinkle with the reserved chocolate crunch.

iii. Allow to set at room temperature for 24 hours.

iv. The following day, demould by bending and banging the mould on the work surface. If tempered correctly they should fall straight out and have a shiny surface.

v. Wrap in paper or plastic bags. Store at ambient temperature for up to 12 months.

* for the Chocolate Crunch

200g caster sugar
75g water
80g chocolate, 73% Dominican Republic

i. **For the caramel**: Caramelise the sugar and water to 135°C. Add the chocolate and constantly stir - this will create a granular sandy texture.

50g hazelnuts
Pinch of salt
15g demerara sugar

ii. **For the praline**: Preheat oven to 180°C. Place the hazelnuts, salt and sugar onto a silicone lined baking sheet. Toast for 5-10 minutes, until just golden.

60g white chocolate

iii. **For the caramelised chocolate**: Lay the white chocolate callets onto a silicone sheet and place in the oven for 15 minutes, stirring every 2-3 minutes.

20g cocoa powder
60g olive oil

iv. **For the chocolate oil**: Mix the powder into the oil. Emulsify until smooth.

v. **Build**: in a stainless steel bowl, mix together the caramel, praline, caramelised chocolate and oil. Thoroughly stir and lay flat onto a baking sheet. Allow to cool. Use immediately or transfer to a sterilised jar and store for up to 6 months at room temperature.

Mint and chocolate is a classic combination.

With over 600 varieties of mint, its important to chose the right one to pair with the right chocolate. And what better variety than 'chocolate mint'.

This is known by its distinctive chocolate brown coloured stem and brown-green leaves. It smells similar to spearmint and tastes of after dinner mints!

It's so easy to grow in your garden and perfect for chocolate bars, truffles and mint cacao tea! Just remember to plant in a pot and never plant different mint varieties together, because as soon as their roots touch, they will taste identical!

fruit & nut 55%

Makes approx. 6 x 60g bars

The Cadbury family were one of the first chocolatiers to create this classic combination. The bar was first launched in 1926 using their Dairy Milk chocolate.

My version uses a very fruity 55% Dominican Republic chocolate. This is married perfectly with juicy flame raisins, unsulphured apricots and the finest Piedmont hazelnuts.

Its worth splashing out on some delicious fruit and nuts as they are generally so plump and full of flavour!

400g 55% dark chocolate
18 flame raisins
6 natural cherries
6 unsulphered apricots
18 hazelnuts

i.   Temper the chocolate (*see page 19*).

ii. Pour into a polished mould. Push the dried fruits and nuts into the top of the bars.

iii. Allow to set at room temperature for 24 hours.

iv. The following day, demould by bending and banging the mould on the work surface. If tempered correctly they should fall straight out and have a shiny surface.

v.   Wrap in paper or plastic bags. Store at ambient temperature for up to 12 months.

Eton mess

Makes approx. 6 x 60g bars

400g white chocolate
1tbsp freeze dried raspberries
2 meringue nests
1tsp vanilla seeds

i. Temper the chocolate (*see page 19*)

ii. Pour into a polished mould. Sprinkle the crushed meringue pieces and raspberries on top and finish with a swirl of white chocolate.

iii. Allow to set at room temperature for 24 hours.

iv. The following day, demould by bending and banging the mould on the work surface. If tempered correctly, they should fall straight out and have a shiny surface.

v. Wrap in paper or plastic bags. Store at ambient temperature for up to 12 months.

Believed to have originated at Eton College in 1893,
this dessert is quintessentially British.

Use a 'real' white chocolate for maximum flavour and ultimate creaminess.
White chocolate should only contain cocoa butter, milk, sugar and possibly vanilla.
Steer clear if it contains vegetable fats or palm oil!

I developed this particular bar in celebration of
Queen Elizabeth II's Diamond Jubilee in the summer of 2012.

Daniel Jones

Artisan Chocolatier
& Patissier

Eton Mess

A creamy white chocolate bar
with textures of raspberry & meringue

The Diamond Jubilee Collection

red peppercorn & ruby snaps

Makes 4 x 100g bags of shards

Ruby chocolate was introduced in 2017 by Barry Callebaut. It is made with unfermented cocoa beans, resulting in a natural pink colour and a complex fruity and acidic taste.

Known as the 'King of Pepper', Kampot red peppercorns have a distinctive and highly aromatic sweet fruity profile with a warm underlying heat.

400g ruby chocolate
1tsp Kampot red peppercorns

i. Temper the chocolate (*see page 19*)

ii. Spread out with a palette knife onto a silicone mat.

iii. Using a pepper grinder, grind the peppercorns evenly over the top.

iv. Allow to set at room temperature for 24 hours.

v. The following day, snap into shards. If tempered correctly they should fall straight out and have a shiny surface.

vi. Wrap in paper or plastic bags. Store at ambient tempera-

filled
chocolates

passionfruit

Makes approx. 24 chocolates

Passionfruit is one of my favourite tropical fruits, zingy, sharp and refreshing.

It pairs very well with a fruity chocolate. I won Gold and Silver awards for this chocolate and it was also served at my own wedding!

50g passionfruit puree
20g water
10g sugar syrup
20g cane sugar
15g glucose
40g white chocolate

To make the ganache:

i. Heat the passionfruit puree, water, sugar and glucose in a heavy based pan. Heat to 120°C.

ii. Remove from heat and allow to cool for 10 minutes.

iii. Add the chocolate to the hot passionfruit mixture. Stir well to emulsify. Transfer to a Tupperware container and cover. Store at ambient temperature overnight or until ready to use.

iv. Alternatively, pour the mixture into sterilised jars and store in the fridge for up to 6 months. Spread on toast or use as a filling in a cake!

500g white chocolate, for tempering

To make the chocolate shells:

i. Temper the chocolate (*see page 19*) and pour into moulds. Make shells by turning mould upside down for 5 minutes. Turn over and scrape the edge clean. Allow to set fully.

ii. Pipe in the passionfruit ganache and cap with tempered chocolate. After 24 hours, remove the chocolates from the moulds and store at room temperature for up to 6 months.

lemongrass & malibu

Makes approx. 24 chocolates

This recipe was inspired by a cocktail that I had whilst sitting on Crane Beach in Barbados, the home of rum distilling!

Made with fresh sugar cane juice, coconut and aromatic lemongrass, it was incredibly perfumed. This works incredibly well with a creamy milk chocolate. I would recommend a 40% St Lucian chocolate as this has underlying coconut and fruity notes.

40g coconut milk
20g cane sugar or coconut nectar
5g lemongrass

To make the infusion:

i. Gently heat the coconut milk, sugar and lemongrass in a heavy based pan. Once at a simmer, remove from heat and allow to cool and infuse for 2 hours at room temperature.

85g milk chocolate
5g malibu

To make the ganache:

i. Gently heat up the liquor until just warm. Add the Malibu.

ii. Melt the chocolate either in a bain marie or microwave. Pour the liquor over the melted chocolate and mix well until thoroughly combined. Store in the fridge for a minimum of 4 hours.

500g 37% milk chocolate, for tempering

To make the chocolate shells:

i. Temper the chocolate (*see page 19*) and pour into moulds. Make shells by turning mould upside down for 5 minutes. Turn over and scrape the edge clean. Allow to set fully.

ii. Pipe in the lemongrass ganache and cap with tempered chocolate. After 24 hours, remove the chocolates from the moulds and store at room

strawberry & pink peppercorn

Makes approx. 24 chocolates

60g cream
200g strawberry puree
8g pink peppercorn

To make the infusion:

i.   Gently heat the cream, puree and peppercorns. Heat to about 80°C. Pour into a sterilised jar and seal with a lid. Refrigerate for 24 hours.

ii. Pour the infusion through a piece of muslin and press to release the liquor – you should get 125g of liquor back. Discard the pink peppercorns.

110g white chocolate

To make the ganache:

i.   Gently heat up the liquor until just warm. Melt the chocolate either in a bain marie or microwave. Pour the liquor over the melted chocolate and mix well until thoroughly combined. Store in the fridge for a minimum of 4 hours.

500g white chocolate

To make the chocolate shells:

i.   Temper the chocolate (*see page 19*) and pour into moulds. Make shells by turning mould upside down for 5 minutes. Turn over and scrape the edge clean. Allow to set fully.

ii. Pipe in the strawberry ganache and cap with tempered chocolate. After 24 hours, remove the chocolates from the moulds and store at room temperature for up to 2 weeks.

blueberry & liquorice

Liquorice can be used for flavour (think intense aniseed) but can also be used for mouthfeel and intense sweetness. The active compound found in liquorice, glycyrrhizic acid, is up to 50 times sweeter that white sugar and gives the most incredible long creamy sweet finish.

It is balanced here with slightly sharp, but sweet blueberries. The white chocolate will help with the creaminess of the ganache, and a dark chocolate will bring the whole recipe alive. Try a rich and fruity Vietnamese chocolate!

160g blueberry puree
80g water
10g date nectar
10g cane sugar
70g glucose
16g liquorice

To make the infusion:

i. Heat the blueberry, water, date nectar, sugar and glucose in a heavy based pan, until all has dissolved. Remove from the heat and add the liquorice. Leave at ambient temperature for 24 hours.

85g white chocolate

To make the ganache:

i. The next day, strain the mixture through a piece of muslin cloth and transfer to a saucepan. You should have around 200g of liquor left.

ii. Heat the liquor to 120°C. the mixture should reduce by about half.

iii. Remove from heat and allow to cool for 10 minutes.

iv. Add the chocolate to the hot blueberry mixture. Stir well to emulsify. Transfer to a Tupperware container and cover. Store at ambient temperature overnight or until ready to use.

500g 80% dark chocolate

To make the chocolate shells:

i. Temper the chocolate (*see page 19*) and pour into moulds. Make shells by turning mould upside down for 5 minutes. Turn over and scrape the edge clean. Allow to set fully.

ii. Pipe in the passionfruit ganache and cap with tempered chocolate. After 24 hours, remove the chocolates from the moulds and store at room temperature for up to 6 months.

pink elderflower & rose

Makes approx. 24 chocolates

40g champagne
30g soda water
6g rose petals

To make the infusion:

i. Mix together the champagne, water and rose petals in a glass bowl. Cover and leave at ambient temperature to infuse for 12 hours.

ii. Pour the infusion through a piece of muslin and press to release the liquor. You should get about 50g of liquor back. Discard the rose petals.

120g white chocolate

To make the ganache:

i. Gently heat up the liquor until just warm. Melt the chocolate either in a bain marie or microwave. Pour the liquor over the melted chocolate and mix well until combined. Store in the fridge for a minimum of 4 hours.

500g white chocolate
24 dried rose petals
for garnishing

To make the chocolate shells:

i. Temper the chocolate (*see page 19*) and pour into moulds. Make shells by turning mould upside down for 5 minutes. Turn over and scrape the edge clean. Allow to set fully.

ii. Pipe in the rose ganache and cap with tempered chocolate. After 24 hours, remove the chocolates from the moulds and decorate with a single dried rose petal on top of each one. Stick them on with a little melted white

My favourite pink elderflowers include Chocolate Marzipan (for a nutty flavour), Black Beauty (for a floral fruity flavour) or Blackcurrant (for an intense blackcurrant flavour)

salted caramel

Sweet and salty senses are complete opposites - and if you add more of one it enhances the other. Add a pinch of brine salt to a caramel or ganache and it instantly brings out the flavour!

Salted caramels date back to the late 1970's when chocolatier Henri Le Roux used the famous salted butter from Brittany to create his delectable delights.

45g cane sugar
70g demerara
45g butter
110g golden syrup
50g cream
1g Droitwich Spa brine salt

To make the caramel:

i.   In a heavy based pan, heat the sugars, butter and golden syrup until dissolved. Continue to simmer over a low heat until 121°C is reached.

ii.   Slowly pour in the cream and bring to the boil for 2 minutes. Be careful as the sugar may spit a little when adding the cream. Season with the salt.

iii.   Transfer to a tupperware container and allow to cool at ambient temperature.

500g 80% dark chocolate

To make the chocolate shells:

i.   Temper the chocolate (*see page 19*) and pour into moulds. Make shells by turning mould upside down for 5 minutes. Turn over and scrape the edge clean. Allow to set fully.

ii.   Pipe in the salted caramel (about 7g per chocolate) and cap with tempered chocolate. After 24 hours, remove the chocolates from the moulds store at room temperature

truffles

70g water
2tbsp freeze dried coffee granules
2tbsp freshly ground coffee
2tbsp cascara husk

For the infusion:

i.   Melt the chocolate to 35°C.

ii.   Heat the water to 70°C and infuse the coffee granules, coffee grounds and cascara for 10 minutes. Drain, reserving the infused liquor and about 2tsp of the used coffee grounds. Set 1tsp of coffee grounds aside for garnishing.

160g 73% dark chocolate

For the ganache:

i.   Pour the warm water over the melted chocolate and stir to emulsify. Add the used coffee grounds and stir. Pour into a container and chill in the fridge overnight.

250g 73% dark chocolate

Make the truffles:

i.   The following day weigh and roll the coffee ganache into 10g balls. Use your fingers rather than the palms of your hands as they are cooler. Place neatly onto a silicone lined tray.

ii.   Temper the chocolate (*see page 19*)

2tsp used coffee grounds (from ganache)

Coat the truffles:
there are two ways to do this, either:

i.   Place a small amount of tempered chocolate on the palm of one hand. Roll the truffle around with your other hand. Place back on silicone lined tray and garnish with a pinch of used coffee grounds. Allow to set at room temperature for at least 3 hours, or overnight.

Or:

i.   Use a dipping fork to dip the truffles into the tempered chocolate. Tap on side of bowl to remove excess chocolate and place back on silicone lined tray. Garnish with a pinch of used coffee grounds. Allow to set at room temperature for at least 3 hours, or overnight.

Enjoy and eat within 1 week! If fully sealed with tempered chocolate they will be fine to store at room temperature for up to 1 week.

If there are slight air gaps, storing them in the fridge is best, although they will have a tendency to lose their shine.

Coffee Cherry Tea is rarely drunk in the UK, but in coffee growing nations, this is a daily ritual. It is made by brewing dried coffee cherries, or cascara, exactly how we would with coffee beans. The difference is cascara is sweeter and incredibly fruity!

Pairing cascara with coffee takes a standard truffle to the next level.

Remember coffee is very similar to cacao. Depending on where it grows in the world will dictate its incredible flavour profile.

mojito

60g double cream
9g lime zest (1 lime)
12g fresh Mojito mint leaves

For the infusion:

i.   Heat the cream to 70°C and infuse with the lime zest, and mint. Leave to infuse in the fridge overnight.

180g 37% milk chocolate
30g Mount Gay rum
9g lime juice (1/4 lime)
2 drops garden mint essential oil

For the ganache:

i.   Melt the chocolate to 35°C.

ii. Drain the infused cream, reserving the liquor. Gently heat to 50°C. Remove from heat and add the rum and lime juice.

iii. Pour the warm liquor over the melted chocolate and stir to emulsify. Add the mint oil and stir. Pour into a container and chill in the fridge overnight.

1tsp dried mint leaves
250g 73% dark chocolate

Make the truffles:

i.   The following day weigh and roll the ganache into 10g balls. Use your fingers rather than the palms of your hands as they are cooler. Place neatly onto a silicone lined tray.

ii. Temper the chocolate (*see page 19*).

Coat the truffles:
there are two ways to do this, either:

i.   Place a small amount of tempered chocolate on the palm of one hand. Roll the truffle around with your other hand. Place back on silicone lined tray and garnish with a pinch of dried mint leaves. Allow to set at room temperature for at least 3 hours, or overnight.

Or:

i.   Use a dipping fork to dip the truffles into the tempered chocolate. Tap on side of bowl to remove excess chocolate and place back on silicone lined tray. Garnish with a pinch of dried mint leaves. Allow to set at room temperature for at least 3 hours, or overnight.

The authentic mint to make this famous cocktail is called Mojito Mint, or Yerba Buena.

It originated in Cuba and the mild, warm mints is enhanced by citrus, sugar and rum. I use dark Mount Gay Rum to give more of a caramel edge.

Enjoy and eat within 2 weeks! If fully sealed with tempered chocolate they will be fine to store at room temperature for up to 2 weeks.

If there are slight air gaps, storing them in the fridge is best, although they will have a tendency to lose their shine.

peanut butter

90g 40% milk chocolate
130g crunchy salted peanut butter
45g butter
10g maple syrup

For the ganache:

i. Melt the chocolate to 35°C.

ii. Soften the butter and add the maple syrup and peanut butter. Beat until smooth. Add the melted chocolate to the peanut butter and stir well until all combined. Pour into a container and chill in the fridge overnight.

Make the truffles:

i. The following day weigh and roll the ganache into 10g balls. Use your fingers rather than the palms of your hands as they are cooler. Place neatly onto a silicone lined tray.

ii. Temper the chocolate (*see page 19*).

250g 40% milk chocolate

Coat the truffles:
there are two ways to do this, either:

i. Place a small amount of tempered chocolate on the palm of one hand. Roll the truffle around with your other hand. Place back on silicone lined tray. Allow to set at room temperature for at least 3 hours, or overnight.

Or:

i. Use a dipping fork to dip the truffles into the tempered chocolate. Tap on side of bowl to remove excess chocolate and place back on silicone lined tray. Allow to set at room temperature for at least 3 hours, or overnight.

Enjoy and eat within 2 weeks!

If fully sealed with tempered chocolate they will be fine to store at room temperature for up to 2 weeks. If there are slight air gaps, storing them in the fridge is best, although they will have a tendency to lose their shine.

This is one of the simplest truffles to make, and equally one of the tastiest.

Choose your favourite milk chocolate and your favourite peanut butter and literally mix them together! I like to use a 'smunchy' peanut butter, half crunchy for texture and half smooth for creaminess.

Similar to chocolate, the use of peanuts actually dates back to the Meso-American era, where they were used as a toothache remedy!

Theobroma cacao literally translates as 'food of the gods'. So this truffle uses all parts of this fabulous fruit to celebrate its origins.

The nibs give texture and a slight bitterness, the husk gives a unique earthiness and the chocolate gives the mouthfeel and sweetness.

The word chocolate is believed to have been derived from the Aztec word 'xocolatl', meaning bitter water. So by using water instead of cream, it is not only authentic, but also allows the flavour of the chocolate to shine!

food of the gods

Makes approx. 24 truffles

120g water	**For the infusion**:
3tbsp cacao nibs	i. Heat the water to 100°C and infuse with the caca nibs and husk for 1 hour.
3tbsp cacao husks	

150g 70% dark chocolate

For the ganache:

i.   Melt the chocolate to 35°C. Drain the infusion - you should end up with approximately 25g liquor. Add this to the chocolate and emulsify. Pour into a container and chill in the fridge overnight.

Make the truffles:

i.   The following day weigh and roll the ganache into 10g balls. Use your fingers rather than the palms of your hands as they are cooler. Place neatly onto a silicone lined tray.

ii.   Temper the chocolate (*see page 19*).

250g 85% dark chocolate
3tbsp cacao nibs, crushed

Coat the truffles:
there are two ways to do this, either:

i.   Place a small amount of tempered chocolate on the palm of one hand. Roll the truffle around with your other hand. Place back on silicone lined tray and garnish with a pinch of crushed cacao nibs. Allow to fully set at room temperature for at least 3 hours, or overnight.

Or:

i.   Use a dipping fork to dip the truffles into the tempered chocolate. Tap on side of bowl to remove excess chocolate and place back on silicone lined tray. Garnish with a pinch of crushed cacao nibs. Allow to fully set at room temperature for at least 3 hours, or overnight.

Enjoy and eat within 1 week! If fully sealed with tempered chocolate they will be fine to store at room temperature for up to 1 week.

If there are slight air gaps, storing them in the fridge is best, although they will have a tendency to lose their shine.

This combines three of my favourite varieties of mint, balancing aromatic floral notes with fiery pepperiness. Perfect for an after dinner treat!

three mint

Makes approx. 24 truffles

180g water
12g fresh garden mint
8g fresh field mint
4g fresh chocolate mint

For the infusion:

i.   Place the mint into cold water and leave at ambient temperature for 24 hours.

220g 55% dark chocolate

For the ganache:

i.   Melt the chocolate to 35°C.

ii.   Drain the infusion, discarding the mint. Heat to 50°C and add this to the chocolate. Stir and emulsify. Pour into a container and chill in the fridge overnight.

Make the truffles:

i.   The following day weigh and roll the ganache into 10g balls. Use your fingers rather than the palms of your hands as they are cooler. Place neatly onto a silicone lined tray.

ii.   Temper the chocolate (*see page 19*).

250g 55% dark chocolate
4tsp dried mint leaves

Coat the truffles:

there are two ways to do this, either:

i.   Place a small amount of tempered chocolate on the palm of one hand. Roll the truffle around with your other hand. Place back on silicone lined tray and garnish with a pinch of dried mint leaves. Allow to fully set at room temperature for at least 3 hours, or overnight.

Or:

i.   Use a dipping fork to dip the truffles into the tempered chocolate. Tap on side of bowl to remove excess chocolate and place back on silicone lined tray. Garnish with a pinch of dried mint leaves. Allow to fully set at room temperature for at least 3 hours, or overnight.

Enjoy and eat within 1 week! If fully sealed with tempered chocolate they will be fine to store at room temperature for up to 1 week.

If there are slight air gaps, storing them in the fridge is best, although they will have a tendency to lose their shine.

rapeseed oil & dukkha

Makes approx. 24 chocolates

½ tsp cumin seed
1tsp coriander seed
2tsp sesame seed
1/4tsp chilli flakes
¼ tsp sea salt
1/4tsp mint, dried
50g hazelnuts

For the dukkha:

i. Crush all of the ingredients in a pestle and mortar until a fine spice blend is achieved. Use as required or store in a sterilised jar for up to 3 months.

100g 73% dark chocolate
100g double cream
48g unrefined olive oil
20g date nectar
20g dukkha
2g fresh mint, chopped

For the ganache:

i. Melt the chocolate to 35°C.

ii. Heat the cream and date nectar to 50°C and emulsify with the chocolate. Stir in the oil, dukkha and freshly chopped mint. Pour into a container and chill in the fridge overnight.

250g 73% dark chocolate
1 tsp dukkha

Make the truffles:

i. The following day weigh and roll the ganache into 10g balls. Use your fingers rather than the palms of your hands as they are cooler. Place neatly onto a silicone lined tray.

ii. Temper the chocolate (*see page 19*).

Coat the truffles:
there are two ways to do this, either:

i. Place a small amount of tempered chocolate on the palm of one hand. Roll the truffle around with your other hand. Place back on silicone lined tray and garnish with a pinch of dukkha. Allow to fully set at room temperature for at least 3 hours, or overnight.

Or:

i. Use a dipping fork to dip the truffles into the tempered chocolate. Tap on side of bowl to remove excess chocolate and place back on silicone lined tray. Garnish with a pinch of dukkha. Allow to fully set at room temperature for at least 3 hours, or overnight.

Enjoy and eat within 1 week! If fully sealed with tempered chocolate they will be fine to store at room temperature for up to 1 week.

If there are slight air gaps, storing them in the fridge is best, although they will have a tendency to lose their shine.

Dukkha is an Egyptian blend of nuts, seeds and spices.
This condiment is traditionally used as
a dip with oil and bread.

The dukkha gives an incredibly complex and
unique flavour, as well as a fabulous texture. You can
make the dukkha well in advance and store in a jar,
using it to make truffles, stir into risottos or dip your
bread into!

Not technically a truffle, but it has a similar texture and
can be enrobed in chocolate.

It may sound a little odd, but if you like fudge
you have to try it.

The parsnip gives an incredible rich sweetness to the fudge
and really enhances the texture.

parsnip fudge

125g parsnips (about 2 average sized parsnips)

For the parsnip puree:

i. Peel and dice the parsnips. Boil in a pan of salted water until tender. Drain and blitz in a mixer. Set aside until required.

275g cream
275g cane sugar
45g golden syrup
125g icing sugar

For the fudge:

i. Meanwhile, place the cream, sugar and syrup into a copper pan. Heat to 120°C. Remove from heat. Add the parsnip puree and stir well.

ii. Place mixture into a mixer bowl and fit a paddle attachment. Place on slow speed for 5 minutes.

iii. Slowly add the icing sugar a spoon at a time, and continue to slowly mix for 15 minutes. This process is known as 'fudging' and is what creates the desired texture.

iv. Pour onto a silicone lined tray, approximately 30 x 30cm. Allow to set at room temperature for 24 hours.

250g 65% dark chocolate

Make the truffles:

i. The following day cut the fudge into squares, approximately 20mm square. Place neatly onto a silicone lined tray.

ii. Temper the chocolate (see page 19).

Coat the truffles:
there are two ways to do this, either:

i. Place a small amount of tempered chocolate on the palm of one hand. Roll the truffle around with your other hand. Place back on silicone lined tray. Allow to fully set at room temperature for at least 3 hours, or overnight.

Or:

i. Use a dipping fork to dip the truffles into the tempered chocolate. Tap on side of bowl to remove excess chocolate and place back on silicone lined tray. Allow to fully set at room temperature for at least 3 hours, or overnight.

Enjoy and eat within 4 weeks! If fully sealed with tempered chocolate they will be fine to store at room temperature for up to 4 weeks.

Brazilian brigadeiro

Makes approx. 30 chocolates

50g unsalted butter
400g tin condensed milk
200g sugar
60g Peruvian cacao powder
pinch of salt
pinch of vanilla seeds
icing sugar, cacao powder or
cacao nibs to decorate

i. Add all ingredients to a large saucepan.

ii. Bring to the boil and then simmer very gently for 10 minutes until thickened (similar to the consistency of fudge). Stir continuously to avoid burning on the bottom. Take care as the mixture will bubble and it will be extremely hot.

iii. Pass through a sieve to remove any lumps. Refrigerate for 1-2 hours until firm. Roll into small truffle sized balls and roll through cacao powder, icing sugar or cacao nibs.

iv. Store in the fridge for up to 7 days.

salame de chocolate

Makes 1 salami log (about 20 slices)

Eaten as a dessert across Portugal, Romania and Italy, this is a delicious treat to keep in the fridge and serve with an espresso when guests come around! It's a real conversation starter!

75g butter	
30g sugar	
1 egg yolk	
10g cacao powder	
50g milk chocolate	
50g dark chocolate	
40g savoury oat biscuits	
20g almonds	
20g walnuts	
10g pecans	
10g desiccated coconut	
10g cacao nibs	
50g apricot	
1 tsp icing sugar	

i. Melt the butter. Add the egg yolk, sugar, cacao powder and chocolate. Heat gently over a bain marie until melted and smooth.

ii. Add the remaining ingredients, except for the icing sugar, to the melted chocolate mixture. Pour into a glass dish and allow to set for 30 minutes.

iii. Spoon the firm mixture onto a sheet of silicone paper. Roll and shape into the shape of a salami sausage, with roughened edges. Allow to fully set for a minimum of 3 hours.

iv. Remove from paper and rub icing sugar over the outside, ensuing not to fully cover.

v. Tie some butchers string around to make it look like a salami sausage. Rewrap in silicone paper and store in the fridge for up to 7 days.

vi. Slice off as necessary and serve alongside an espresso.

macarons

Macaron (not to be confused with macaroon) is a meringue based patisserie often served at an afternoon tea. They have a long history dating back to the 8th century, although it wasn't until the 1830s that the macaron was served as we know them today – two shells filled with a frosting, ganache or curd.

75g ground almonds
75g icing sugar
1 egg white

75g sugar
25g water
1 egg white

i. Sieve together the almonds and icing sugar.

ii. Add the egg white and mix until combined. Set aside.

iii. Heat the sugar and water in a heavy based (preferably copper) pan. Heat to 120°C. Do not be tempted to stir, just swirl the pan around. If you stir it will crystallise.

iv. While the sugar is boiling, whisk the egg whites with a mixer. Once the sugar has reached temperature slowly pour over the whisked egg white whisk on slow speed. Continue to whisk until cool.

v. Fold one third of the meringue mixture into the almond mixture. Once carefully combined, fold in the remaining two thirds. Once combined fold carefully for a further 15 times. This is the macaronnage stage and is critical to achieving the correct sheen and texture.

vi. Transfer to a piping bag and pipe 24 circles onto a silicone sheet, approximately 25mm in diameter. Bang the baking sheet firmly against the counter. Allow to rest, uncovered for 30 minutes. This is a critical stage which allows the pied to form.

vii. Bake for 12 minutes at 160°C. Allow to cool on silicone mat before removing.

viii. Set aside.

ix. Once cooled, pipe half of the shells with the filling of your choice.

Recipe Ideas

Liquorice & Vanilla

Lemon Curd & Poppyseed

Rose & Pink Elderflower

Mint & Matcha Tea

Peach Melba

Salted Peanut Butter

Banana & Rum

Passionfruit

(use any of the flavours from the infusions or truffles sections of this book)

the filling

Frosting
300g icing
100g butter
25g milk or yoghurt
Infusion or flavouring

i.   In a mixer, beat the icing sugar and butter together until light and fluffy.

ii. Slowly add the milk and flavouring (*see ideas on opposite page*) and beat for 5 minutes.

For a chocolate filling:
i.   Replace 50g of the icing sugar with cocoa powder.

For a cream cheese filling:
i.   Half the amount of butter and add 100g of cream cheese.

Ganache
100g white chocolate
50g double cream
50g infusion, optional

For a ganache filling:
i.   Emulsify your cream, infusion and chocolate. (*see page 18*)

Curd
75g butter or cocoa butter
100g caster sugar
2 lemons (juice and zest)
3 eggs, sieved
25g white chocolate

Curd can be a tricky and time consuming thing to make. This fool proof recipe has been passed down through family generations (now tweaked with a chocolate twist!) and will only take you 10 minutes to make!

i.   In a microwavable glass bowl, whisk together the sugar and eggs. Add the citrus juice, zest and diced butter.

ii. Cook in the microwave on full power for approximately 6-7 minutes, stirring every minute. Once finished, it should coat the back of a wooden spoon. Add in the chocolate and stir until emulsified.

iii. Pour into sterilised jars and store in the fried for

dough,
cakes
& bakes

chocolate sourdough

**Makes 1
rustic loaf**

200g leaven
180g strong white flour
150g rye flour
225g water

The day before:

i.   Mix the leaven with the flours and water. Leave in a warm place for 24 hours. You can leave for up to 48 hours for a more 'sour' taste.

170g wholemeal bread flour
50g dark rye flour
30g strong white flour
10g salt
10g yeast
approx. 100g water

The following morning:

i.   Mix the flours in a bowl. Add the yeast to one side and the salt to the other. Slowly add the cold water and mix until combined and a nice dough is formed.

ii.   Work the gluten by kneading for 10 minutes. Return to a clean oiled bowl and leave to prove all day (whilst at work).

50g 55% dark chocolate
100g hazelnuts
100g flame rains

Later that evening:

i.   Knock back the dough. Add the chocolate, raisins and hazelnuts and mix through by hand.

ii.   Shape the dough into rounds and either place into an oiled tin or a proving basket. Loosely cover with a tea towel. Return to a warm place overnight (up to 8 hours).

A leaven , also called a starter, is 50:50 flour and water.

I prefer to use rye flour. Mix together, feeding the mixture with 1tbsp of flour and water each day. Use after one week. Keep feeding and it will live forever!

The following morning:

i.   Preheat the oven to 240°C and place in a baking sheet to heat up.

ii.   Once oven is up to temperature, turn the dough out from the proving basket onto the hot tray. Slash the top of the loaf and bake for 25 minutes.

iii.   Reduce the temperature to 200°C and bake for a further 10 minutes, until cooked through.

iv.   Once cooked, remove from oven and cool on a wire rack. Slice when cool, spread with chocolate spread and enjoy!

chocolate soda bread

Makes 1 tin loaf

With an Irish grandad, I was brought up on delicious traditional soda bread as a child. Ireland's most famous bread is very easy to make and has a distinctive sour and malty taste - perfect to pair with salted butter, mature cheddar and of course cacao!

230g white bread flour
220g wholemeal bread flour
30g cocoa powder
1tsp salt
1sp bicarbonate of soda
200g natural yoghurt
100g leaven*
25g 60% dark chocolate
oats, for garnish

Preheat the oven to 200°C. Mix the flours, oats, cocoa powder, salt and bicarbonate of soda together in a bowl. Mix in the yoghurt, starter and chocolate. Mix until combined (no need to knead!). Transfer to an oiled loaf tin and sprinkle with rolled oats.

Place in the oven and throw in a small cup of water directly onto the base of the over. This will create steam (but do it quickly and be careful of the steam!). Close the door immediately. Bake for 45-55 minutes.

Remove from the tin and allow to cool on a wire rack. Cover with a tea towel to keep the crust soft.

Cupcakes got their names from both baking in cups and using measuring cups to weigh out the ingredients. Today these sweet treats are flavoured and filled with all sorts of interesting combinations.

This is a super-sonic chocolate filled version. Chocolate sponge, praline filling, ganache frosting and topped with white, milk and dark chocolate!
A real chocolate indulgence.

chocolate praline cupcakes

Makes approx. 12 cupcakes

45g butter
125g caster sugar
1 whole egg
100g whole milk
Pinch of salt
Pinch vanilla paste
90g plain flour
35g cocoa powder
2tsp baking powder
30g 37% milk chocolate buttons

i. Preheat the oven to 180°C. In a mixer, cream the butter and sugar with the beater attachment. Once creamy, change over to the whisk attachment and whisk in the eggs and milk.

ii. Slowly whisk in the salt, vanilla, flour, cocoa powder and baking powder. Once all combined, fold the milk chocolate buttons in by hand.

iii. Line a 12-hole cupcake tray with paper cases. Spoon the mixture into the cases, only filling two thirds full.

iv. Bake for 20-25 minutes until cooked through.

v. Remove from oven and allow to cool on a baking wire.

275g icing sugar
100g salted butter, softened
50g cocoa powder
35g whole milk

Make the frosting:

i. Put all of the ingredients into a mixing bowl. Gently whisk until mostly combined and then continue to whisk on fast speed until fluffy, approximately 5 minutes. Set aside until ready to use.

60g choco-nut spread
(*see page 148*)
chopped white, milk and
dark chocolate for garnish

Build the cakes:

i. Spoon the choco-nut spread into a piping bag.

ii. Once the cakes are cool, use a small circular cutter to remove a section from the centre of the cake. Set aside.

iii. Pipe in a little of the choco-nut spread and top with the removed piece of cake.

iv. Divide the frosting equally between the 12 cakes. Using a small palette knife, build up the outer edges and swirl the centre. If you prefer, you can pipe the mixture onto the cupcakes.

v. Leave plain or top with your favourite toppings, such as grated chocolate or raw cacao nibs. Store at ambient temperature for up to 5 days.

banana & chocolate loaf

Makes approx. 1 tin loaf

4 ripe bananas
140g salted butter
250g soft brown sugar
2 eggs
250g plain flour
1tsp baking powder
200g 40% milk chocolate

i.   Pre heat the oven to 180°C.

ii.   Roughly mash the bananas with a fork. Set aside.

iii. In a separate bowl, beat the butter and sugar until creamy. Slowly add the eggs one at a time, followed by the sieved flour and baking powder.

iv.   Mix in the banana puree and chocolate chips.

v.   Transfer mixture to a lined loaf tin (11 x 22 x 7cm).

vi.   Bake in the preheated oven for 40-45 minutes, or until cooked through and golden.

vii. Remove from oven and allow to cool in the tin for 1 hour.

viii. Remove from tin, completely cool on a cooling wire and store in an airtight tin.

Banana bread actually became popular throughout America in the early 1900s
and there is even a National Banana Bread day in February!

I just enjoy making this with an old banana or two that's a little past its best.
Eat it just warm to enjoy oozing chocolate chips throughout!

white chocolate & tonka bean oaties

Makes approx. 20-24 biscuits

125g salted butter
75g unrefined caster sugar
75g soft brown sugar
1 whole egg
Pinch grated tonka beans
Pinch of salt
1/2tsp baking powder
100g plain flour
100g toasted breadcrumbs
50g jumbo oats
25g cacao nibs
250g white chocolate
tonka beans & cacao nibs,
to decorate

Make the dough in advance:

i.   Beat the butter and sugars together until creamy.

ii.   Add the egg, vanilla and salt. Mix until combined.

iii. Stir in the flour, breadcrumbs, oats and cacao nibs. Mix until all combined. Roll out a sheet of silicone paper and place the dough down the centre. Fold over the paper, rolling the dough as you go to form a log. Twist both end and place in the freezer to firm up. The mixture can be stored in the freezer for up to 6 months.

To bake:

i.   Preheat the oven to 190°C. Remove the dough from the freezer and cut into 5mm slices. Place onto a silicone lined baking sheet and bake for 10-12 minutes, until golden.

ii.   Remove from oven and cool completely on a wire rack.

To decorate:

i.   Temper the chocolate (*see page 19*).

ii.   Dip half of the biscuits into the chocolate. Grate over a tiny amount of tonka bean and sprinkle the cacao nibs before they set.

Tonka beans are one of my favourite spices. The incredibly aromatic notes work brilliantly well with the creamy white chocolate and oatiness of the biscuits. Delicious with or without a cuppa.

Chewy flapjack, puffed rice squares,
salted butterscotch and super soft brownie.
Four of my favourites in one traybake. A must try!

quadrillionaires

For the butterscotch:

65g caster sugar
95g soft brown sugar
65g butter
1/2 tsp salt
160g golden syrup
70g double cream

For the butterscotch:

i. In a heavy bottomed pan, place the butter, golden syrup, sugar and salt, and heat until the sugar has dissolved. Continue to stir until the mixture reaches caramel stage (153°C).

ii. Slowly add in in the cream (but be careful of steam and spitting!). Stir well and bring back to the boil until it is smooth and caramel like. Pour through a sieve onto a silicone lined 20x20cm baking tray. Allow to set overnight in the fridge.

For the puffed rice flapjack:

125g butter
125g golden syrup
100g muscovado sugar
150g rolled oats
50g rice krispies

For the puffed rice flapjack:

i. The following day, heat the butter, syrup and sugar until ingredients have dissolved. Stir in the oats and rice krispies. Pour into a silicone lined 20x20cm tray and flatten until smooth. Bake for 12 minutes at 180°C. Turn out and allow to cool on a wire rack.

For the brownie:

175g cane sugar
1 eggs
125g salted butter, softened
35g cocoa powder
30g plain flour
1tsp baking powder
1tsp vanilla seeds
pinch of salt
125g 35% milk chocolate

For the brownie:

i. Add all of the ingredients, except for the chocolate to a mixing bowl. Whisk on half speed until fluffy. Stir in the chocolate.

ii. Bake in a silicone lined 20x20cm tray for 15 minutes at 180°C. Allow to cool in tray for 15 minutes.

Montage:

i. place the flapjack on a silicone lined baking sheet. Top with the butterscotch from the fridge (this will be flexible).

ii. Whilst the brownie is still just warm, place on top of the butterscotch, sandwiching together.

iii. Place your original 20x20cm baking tray over the top to stop the butterscotch from leaking. Place in the fridge until set. Cut into 16 squares and enjoy at room temperature.

desserts

white chocolate & summer fruit mille feuille

500g ready made puff pastry

For the pastry:

i. Preheat the oven to 230°C.

ii. Roll out the puff pastry to a thickness of 2-3mm. Cut out 18 x 5cm squares and place on a silicone mafta mat. Prick with a fork and sprinkle with a dusting of icing sugar. Place a mafta mat on top and another baking tray. This will allow the pastry to rise just enough.

iii. Bake for 5 minutes, then turn the oven down to 180°C and bake for a further 12-15 minutes, until rich and golden. They will burn very quickly once golden due to the high fat content so don't be tempted to walk away!

iv. Once cooked, golden and crisp, transfer to a cooling wire and dust with icing sugar. Allow to cool fully. Set aside.

500ml whole milk
1 tbsp Tahitian vanilla extract
6 egg yolks
75g caster sugar
25g plain flour
20g cornflour

For the crème patisserie:

i. Beat the milk and vanilla to a gentle simmer. Do not allow to boil.

ii. Whisk the egg yolks and caster sugar until foamy. Whisk in the flour and cornflour.

iii. Add the milk to the egg mixture and whisk. Return to a clean pan and slowly bring to the boil over a gently heat. Whisk continuously until thick (approximately 2-3 minutes). Add the white chocolate and whisk to fully melt. Transfer to a glass bowl and cover with a piece of silicone paper. Allow to cool at room temperature, then store in fridge overnight.

selection of fresh strawberries, raspberries, blackberries & blueberries

Montage (the following day):

i. Slice the berries in half. Melt the white chocolate. Brush 12 of the pastry pieces with white chocolate. Allow to set.

150g double cream

For the crème chiboust:

i. Whisk the cream until soft peaks are formed. Fold the whipped cream into the crème patisserie and transfer to a piping bag.

ii. Using a 5cm square metal ring, begin to layer by placing a piece of chocolate coated pastry on the base. Place the fruit around the outside edge (cut side out) and pipe in the crème patisserie.

iii. Top with another piece of chocolate coated pastry and repeat.

iv. Finally top with the final piece of pastry and dust with icing sugar once more. Enjoy immediately.

So simple, yet so beautiful, and enjoyed with an espresso is a moment of indulgence! It was influenced by the famous chef Marie-Antoine Carême in the 1800's and can now be found in pretty much every patisserie in France.

My version uses the finest summer berries, the most aromatic Tahitian vanilla and the creamiest white chocolate. A perfect summer afternoon treat!

smoked chocolate brownie

Makes approx. 12-18 (depending on size)

Ingredients		Method

350g cane sugar
4 eggs
250g salted butter, softened
75g cocoa powder
60g plain flour
1tsp baking powder
1tsp vanilla seeds
Pinch of salt
250g 60% dark chocolate buttons

i. Preheat your oven or BBQ to 180°C. If you are using an oven place a baking tray on the bottom with woodchips. If you are using a BGE (*see Top Tip below*), setup for indirect cooking in the 'legs-up' position.

ii. Mix all ingredients together in a mixer until smooth.

iii. Fold in the dark chocolate pieces. Pour into a silicone paper lined baking tray (30 x 20cm).

iv. Bake for 25-35 minutes, until just cooked. The centre will still be a little soft, although this will continue cooking when removed from the heat.

v. Allow to cool completely and refrigerate. Cut into squares and gently reheat in the oven, BGE or microwave. Serve with Cacao Nib & Brown Bread Gelato (*see page 125*).

Top Tip:

This always tastes better the following day and its also easier to cut into squares when cool. Store in the fridge for up to a week (if it lasts that long!)

BGE (Big Green Egg)

Anyone who knows me, knows that I am obsessed with my BGE (Big Green Egg). A BGE is a kamado-style ceramic charcoal barbecue cooker, allowing you to grill, bake, roast or smoke.

The best way to bake this brownie is on an BGE or BBQ, as you really get a good smoky depth. But you can always bake in the oven if you prefer.

I couldn't write a chocolate book and not include a staple brownie recipe.
A real brownie, in my opinion, should be crunchy on the outside and super soft in the middle. This version has a subtle smoky background note too, complementing and enhancing the chocolate flavour.

Make ahead before a BBQ, and put on when it is cooling down.
The hot smoke will help it to cook without overcooking it!

You can use any liquor you like to make this. Traditionally Masala is used, which is a sweet wine, although I have opted for Leone 70.

This recipe was inspired after a holiday in the mountains of Tuscany. In the Garfagnana region, a local traditional drink is made which is known as "rum" or "Leone 70". It has an alcohol content of 70% abv and is used to make "Caffè Corretto" or corrected coffee.

tiramisu

50g coffee, ground
30g cacao husk, Panama
400g water
2 tbsp Leone 70

Make the infusion:

i. Place the coffee and cacao husk in a cafetiere. Heat the water to 70°C and pour over. Add the Leone 70 and infuse for 10 minutes. Drain and allow to cool.

80g 55% dark chocolate, melted

Decorate the glasses:

i. Using a palette knife or spoon, decorate the interior of 4 serving classes. Allow to set.

4 eggs
30g caster sugar
2 tbsp Leone 70
200g cream cheese

Make the sabayon:

i. Whisk together the eggs, sugar and Leone 70 over a bain marie. As you whisk, the steam from the bain marie will begin to thicken the mixture. A sabayon is only ready once the whisk leaves a thick trail when lifted. It will be around 55°C, if it gets any hotter the egg will coagulate (or set).

ii. Beat the cream cheese to slacken. Fold one third of the sabayon into the cream cheese. Once combined, carefully fold in the remaining two thirds, taking care not to lose too much air.

16 sponge fingers
40g 60% grated chocolate

Build the desserts:

i. Get everything organised before you being. Sponge fingers next to the infusion on the left hand side of the glasses, cream cheese mixture on the right.

ii. For each glass, soak the sponge fingers on each side for 10 seconds. Layer in the glass with the cream cheese mixture.

iii. Top with grated chocolate and refrigerate for 24 hours.

Dating back to the 1970s, this is now a staple tray bake. I prefer to make individual 'bites' as you get equal quantities of biscuit, caramel and chocolate. Perfect to make on a relaxing Sunday!

millionaires bites

90g butter
50g caster sugar
175g flour
½ tsp baking powder
½ tsp salt
30g cacao nibs
2 egg yolks
25g olive oil

For the biscuit base:

i.   Cream the butter and sugar together until light and fluffy. Rub in the flour, baking powder, salt and cacao nibs until a breadcrumb texture is formed.

ii.   Slowly add the eggs and the oil and mix gently until a dough is formed. Form into a square block and wrap in cling film. Allow to rest in the fridge for 1-2 hours. (You can also form into a log and store in the freezer. Slice off and bake for 12 minutes from frozen for a fresh biscuit!)

iii. Once chilled and firm, roll between two slices of silicone paper until it is approximately 5-8mm thick and fits perfectly in your tray. Place in freezer for 15 minutes. Meanwhile, preheat the oven to 150°C.

iv.   Bake for approximately 15-18 minutes until just golden.

v.   Remove from oven and whilst still warm cut into 4cm square biscuits. Allow to cool on a wire rack and set aside.

90g caster sugar
135g soft brown sugar
90g butter
1tsp salt
225g golden syrup
100g double cream

For the caramel:

i.   In a heavy bottomed pan, place the butter, golden syrup, sugar and salt, and heat until the sugar has dissolved. Continue to stir until the mixture reaches caramel stage (153°C).

ii.   Slowly add in in the cream (but be careful of steam and spitting!) Stir well and bring back to the boil until it is smooth and caramel like. Pour through a sieve onto a silicone lined baking tray. Allow to cool overnight.

iii. Once set, cut into 4cm square pieces. Store on silicone paper and set aside.

300g 73% dark chocolate
20g butter

For the chocolate:

i.   Temper the chocolate (*see page 19*). Add the butter at the end of the process.

Montage:

i.   Place a cooling wire on top of a baking sheet. Place the caramel on top of the   biscuits bases and drizzle over the chocolate. Leave smooth or decorate with cacao nibs for extract crunch!

ii.   Transfer to a silicone lined backing tray and allow to set for 30 minutes. Store in an airtight container for up to 2 weeks.

chocolate & salted pecan tart

Makes approx. 1 x 6" ring

125g pecan nuts

i. Preheat oven to 180°C.

ii. Place nuts onto a baking tray and toast for 5 minutes. Set aside.

125g plain flour
50g salted butter
50g icing sugar
20g cacao nibs
Pinch salt

iii. In a mixing bowl, weigh the flour, butter and sugar. Rub together with your fingertips, but do not overwork.

iv. Add the salt, cacao nibs and egg. Gently mix to form a dough. Wrap in cling film and rest in fridge for 20 minutes.

25g light brown sugar
25g date nectar
30g salted butter
30g double cream
10g cacao nibs
25g white chocolate

v. Meanwhile, bring the sugar, date nectar, butter and cream to the boil. Remove from the heat and fold in the salt, cacao nibs and white chocolate. Add the pecans and set aside.

vi. Roll out the dough to 3mm thick. Line a 6" ring and chill for 15 minutes. Bake for 15 minutes.

vii. Fill with the pecan caramel mixture and return to oven for 20 minutes.

70g whole milk
35g 37% milk chocolate
35g 60% dark chocolate
¼ tsp Himalayan pink salt

viii. To make the ganache, heat the milk to just warm and pour over the chocolate. Season with salt and stir well until emulsified. Set aside.

ix. Once the tart is cooled, pour over the ganache and chill for 2 hours or overnight. Serve with melted dark chocolate, whipped cream and cacao nibs.

chocolate mint

Makes approx. 6 small pots

200g caster sugar
75g water
80g 73% dark chocolate

For the caramel:

i. Caramelise the sugar and water to 135°C. Add the chocolate and constantly stir - this will create a granular sandy texture.

50g hazelnuts
pinch salt
15g demerara sugar

For the praline:

i. Preheat oven to 180°C. Place the hazelnuts, salt and sugar onto a silicone lined baking sheet. Toast for 5-10 minutes, until just golden.

60g white chocolate callets

For the caramelised chocolate:

i. Lay the white chocolate callets onto a silicone sheet and place in the oven for 15 minutes, stirring every 2-3 minutes.

20g cocoa powder
60g olive oil

For the chocolate soil:

i. Mix the powder into the oil. Emulsify until smooth. Mix with the caramelised white chocolate, praline and caramel. Store in an airtight jar until required.

Build:

i. To make the mint pots, make a batch of chocolate mousse (*see page 117*), making a mint infusion with the milk and cream first.

ii. Pour the mousse into clean terracotta pots. Top with the edible soil.

iii. Garnish with a large sprig of chocolate mint.

blood orange 'jaffa cake'

Makes approx. 1 x 20cm round tin

This is my version of the classic McVitie snack. Jaffa Cakes are named after the Jaffa orange variety and have been in production since 1927. I have used a blood orange to add a sharper aromatic note, balanced with the dark chocolate.

For the jelly:

200g blood orange juice
25g lemon juice
150g caster sugar
8g pectin

15g orange puree
5g lemon juice
5g orange juice

Make the jelly:

i. Dissolve the sugar into the orange and lemon juice. Transfer to a blender. Whilst on low speed add the pectin. Remove and transfer to a pan. Bring to the boil, stirring continuously.

ii. Remove from heat and refresh with the puree and remaining juices. Pour into a silicone lined lipped tray to set, ensuring it is not deeper than half a centimetre. Place in the fridge overnight to fully set.

iii. Preheat the oven to 150°C.

For the Genoese sponge:

4 eggs
125g caster sugar
75g melted butter
75g plain flour
Pinch vanilla powder

Make the sabayon:

i. Whisk together the eggs and sugar in a large, round bottomed stainless steel bowl over a bain marie. As you whisk, the steam from the bain marie will begin to thicken the mixture. A sabayon is only ready once the whisk leaves a thick trail when lifted. It will be around 55°C, if it gets any hotter the egg will coagulate (or set).

ii. Very carefully fold in the melted butter, flour and vanilla. Pour into a silicone lined baking tray, no thicker than 1cm. Bake for approximately 15 minutes until fully cooked through. Transfer to a cooling wire to fully cool.

For the glaze:

225g 75% dark chocolate
70g salted butter
20g cocoa powder
30g rum

90g glucose syrup
40g water

Make to the glaze:

i. Before you make the glaze, prepare the bases.

ii. You can either make one large jaffa cake or individual ones. Using a circular cutter, cut the sponge to the preferred size. Cut the jelly 1cm smaller than the sponge discs and place on top. Line them all up on a cooling wire. Place on top of a baking tray and set aside.

iii. Melt the chocolate to 35°C. Add the butter and stir to melt.

iv. Make a paste with the cocoa powder and rum. Set aside.

v. Boil the glucose and water for 1 minute. Pour over the rum mixture and stir. Pour this whole mixture in the melted chocolate. Stir until fully emulsified. Allow to cool for 5 minutes and then pour directly over the jaffa cakes, ensuring that all of the edges are covered.

vi. Allow to set

cappuccino chocolate mousse

Makes approx. 6 portions

Coffee and chocolate work incredibly well together. This is a super light mousse but with a real earthy coffee depth. A quick dessert that can be made in advance and kept in coffee mugs in the fridge ahead of any dinner party.

210g egg whites (approx. 6 eggs)
75g caster sugar

i.   In a mixer, whisk the egg whites until soft peaks are formed. Slowly add the sugar whilst still slowly whisking. Once incorporated, whisk on fast for 3-4 minutes. Set aside.

175g double cream

ii. In a separate bowl, whisk the cream to soft peaks. Set aside.

300g 45% dark-milk chocolate

iii. Melt the chocolate to 35°C. Set aside.

10g brandy
75g caster sugar
120g egg yolks (approx. 6 eggs)

Make the sabayon:

i.   Whisk together the eggs and sugar over a bain marie. As you whisk, the steam from the bain marie will begin to thicken the mixture. A sabayon is only ready once the whisk leaves a thick trail when lifted. It will be around 55°C, if it gets any hotter the egg will coagulate (or set).

1 shot of espresso
1bsp freeze dried coffee granules

ii. Dissolve the coffee granules in the espresso. Set aside.

To construct:

i.   Add the coffee to the sabayon. Carefully fold in the chocolate, followed by the cream, followed by the meringue. Be very careful not to lose too much air when folding through the ingredients.

ii. Once mixed, carefully transfer mixture to a glass or plastic container. Cover with a lid and place in the fridge. Allow to set for at least 4 hours or overnight.

chocolate eclairs

Makes approx. 12 eclairs

Traditionally known in France as a *pain a la duchesse*, this patisserie originated in the nineteenth century and was believed to be the inspiration of Marie-Antonin Carême, a French chef and pioneer of grande cuisine.

This version is for purists, but you can make them any flavour you want by changing the filling and topping. Try coffee, Sicilian orange or salted caramel!

If you are feeling adventurous, you can also use all of the techniques below to make beautiful pâte à choux swans. This was the first ever dessert I cooked for my wife, as she loves eclairs (well in the form of "Swan Pâte à Choux")

Preheat the oven to 180°C.

For the choux paste:
125g milk
125g water
100g butter, diced
½ tsp salt
1 tsp caster sugar
150g soft plain flour
4 eggs

Make the choux paste:

i. In a heavy based pan, heat the milk, water, salt and sugar. Bring to the boil and remove from heat. Stir in the flour and beat until combined. Transfer to a mixer with a beater attachment and put on slow speed.

ii. Add the eggs one at a time and then beat on full speed until the bowl is cool to the touch. The mixture should be smooth, shiny and glossy. Transfer to a piping bag fitted with a 3cm nozzle. Pipe onto a silicone lined sheet into lengths of 12cm, leaving a good distance between each one.

For the egg wash:
1 egg
20g milk

iii. Make an egg wash with the remaining egg and milk. Brush the tops of the eclairs with egg wash and bake for 18-20 minutes, until golden and risen.

iv. Remove from oven and put a small hole in the base. This will help keep the shells crisp. Place on a cooling wire rack until cold.

For the crème patisserie:
500ml whole milk
1tsp vanilla extract
6 egg yolks
75g caster sugar
25g plain flour
20g cornflour

Make the crème patisserie:

i. Heat the milk and vanilla to a gentle simmer. Do not allow to boil.

ii. Whisk the egg yolks and caster sugar until foamy. Whisk in the flour and cornflour. Add the milk to the egg mixture and whisk. Return to a clean pan and slowly bring to the boil over a gently heat. Whisk continuously until thick (approximately 2-3 minutes). Transfer to a glass bowl and cover with a piece of silicone paper. Allow to cool at room temperature, then store in fridge overnight.

For the glaze:
100g dark chocolate
30g salted butter
10g cocoa powder
10g dark rum
35g glucose syrup
15g water

Make the glaze:

i. Melt the chocolate over a bain marie to 35°C. Add the butter and stir. Make a paste with the cocoa powder and rum.

ii. Bring the water and glucose to the boil. Remove from heat.

iii. Add the glucose to the paste. Stir. Then add the paste mixture to the chocolate. Stir until combined and glossy.

Montage:

i. Transfer the crème patisserie to a piping bag without a nozzle. Pipe into the choux shells using the hole that was created in the base.

ii. Dip the top of the eclairs into the chocolate glaze and run along the edge of the bowl to remove any excess.

iii. Place on a cooling wire to set. Enjoy immediately or store in the fridge

Persian pavlova

i.   Preheat oven to 110°C. Draw an oval shape (approx. 25 x 35cm) onto a piece of baking parchment.

For the meringue:

140g egg white (approx. 4 eggs)
230g sugar
1tsp vinegar
100g Turkish delight
100g white chocolate

i.   In a clean glass bowl, whisk the egg whites until the form stiff peaks. Gradually add the sugar, followed by the vinegar. Briskly whisk until it is smooth and shiny, approximately 5-6 minutes. Dice the Turkish delight and chocolate. Carefully fold through the meringue.

ii.   Pipe or spoon the meringue around the oval shape. Place into oven for approximately 2 hours. Turn off the heat and leave meringue in the oven to fully dry out for a further 2 hours. This will results in a crispy shell and chewy inside.

150g white chocolate

iii.   Once cool, melt the chocolate and paint onto the top of the meringue. Allow to fully set.

For the chantilly:

300g double cream
2 tbsp icing sugar
1 tbsp rose limoncello (*see page 39*)

i.   Whisk together the cream, icing sugar and rose limoncello, until soft peaks are formed.

Build the dessert:

100g Turkish delight, diced
1 pomegranate (seeds)
25g green pistachio nuts
25g cacao nibs
20g white chocolate
sprig of fresh mint
1 head of fresh rose petals
1 sheet edible gold leaf

i.   Prepare up to 2 hours before you are going to serve. Place the meringue onto the serving platter. Spoon the chantilly onto the top of the meringue.

ii.   Artistically arrange all of the garnishes in the following order: Turkish delight, pomegranate, pistachios, cacao nibs, white chocolate, mint, rose petals and gold leaf.

iii.   Serve immediately or store in the fridge for 2 days.

This magnificent centrepiece is perfect for any celebration. It is so simple to make but looks like you have spent hours beavering away in the kitchen – a real showstopper.

Here I have paired Persian flavours (floral rose, aromatic pistachios) with creamy white chocolate. Traditionally a pavlova is round, but by making it an oval ring, it means everyone gets an equal slice of everything! It also looks a little bit like a Christmas wreath, so perfect for a festive dinner party.

Legend has it that an American chef pulled a chocolate cake out of the oven before it was cooked through and served it as a 'lava cake'. The best things in life are invented by mistake!

If you cook your sabayon first, it means the eggs are fully cooked through as well as creating a light texture. So when you bake them, you only really want to get a crisp shell. The fondants are very rich so enjoy with vanilla ice cream!

chocolate fondant

Makes approx. 8 dariold moulds

For the centre:
200g dark Manjari chocolate
400g double cream
60g butter

Make the centres:

i. Heat the cream to 70°C. Pour over the chocolate to melt and stir to emulsify. Stir in the pieces of butter and stir until melted. Chill in the fridge for 3-4 hours.

ii. Transfer to a piping bag and pipe circles the size of a 2p piece. Place in freezer overnight or until required.

iii. Line dariold mould with a little melted butter and caster sugar. Set aside.

For the fondant:
300g dark Manjari chocolate
200g butter

Melt the chocolate:

i. Preheat oven to 200°C .

ii. Melt the butter and chocolate to 35°C. Set aside.

For the sabayon:
5 whole eggs
3 egg yolks
125g caster sugar

Make the sabayon:

i. Whisk together the eggs and sugar over a bain marie. As you whisk, the steam from the bain marie will begin to thicken the mixture. A sabayon is only ready once the whisk leaves a thick trail when lifted. It will be around 55°C, if it gets any hotter the egg will coagulate (or set).

For the meringue:
3 egg whites
50g caster sugar

For the meringue:

i. In a clean glass bowl, whisk the egg whites until the form stiff peaks. Gradually add the sugar, followed by the vinegar. Briskly whisk until it is smooth and shiny, approximately 5-6 minutes.

60g plain flour

To build:

i. Carefully fold the melted chocolate into the sabayon.

ii. Fold in the flour.

iii. Very carefully, fold in the meringue.

iv. Pipe into the prepared moulds, placing a frozen disk into the centre of each.

v. Place in freezer for 1 hour.

vi. Bake at 200°C for 20 minutes.

vii. Turn out immediately and serve with your preferred ice cream (*see pages 121-126*).

delectable chocolate mousse

Makes approx. 10 portions

400g chocolate,
64% Madagascan
250g double cream
250g whole milk

Make the ganache:

i. Melt chocolate to 35°C.

ii. Heat the milk and cream gently to about 45°C. You can pre-infuse this liquid with any flavour that you like (*see infusions, page 31*).

iii. Stir into the melted chocolate and emulsify with a spatula, until smooth. Set aside.

140g egg yolk (7 egg yolks)
80g caster sugar
100g water

Make the sabayon:

i. Whisk together the eggs, sugar and water in a large, round bottomed stainless steel bowl over a bain marie. As you whisk, the steam from the bain marie will begin to thicken the mixture. A sabayon is only ready once the whisk leaves a thick trail when lifted. It will be around 55°C, if it gets any hotter the egg will coagulate (or set).

ii. Fold one third of the sabayon into the ganache. Once combined, carefully fold in the remaining two thirds, taking care not to lose too much air.

Build the desserts:

i. Pour the mousse into espresso cups or glasses and chill overnight. Use within 3 days.

Top Tip

Use this as a base recipe and change the flavour by making an infusion with the double cream and milk.

The day before required, infuse a few sprigs of chocolate mint, some spices or citrus peel! Strain and use this infusion for the mousse!

Light and creamy, yet dark and delectable.
A simple and classic dessert that you can
flavour with any infusion you like.

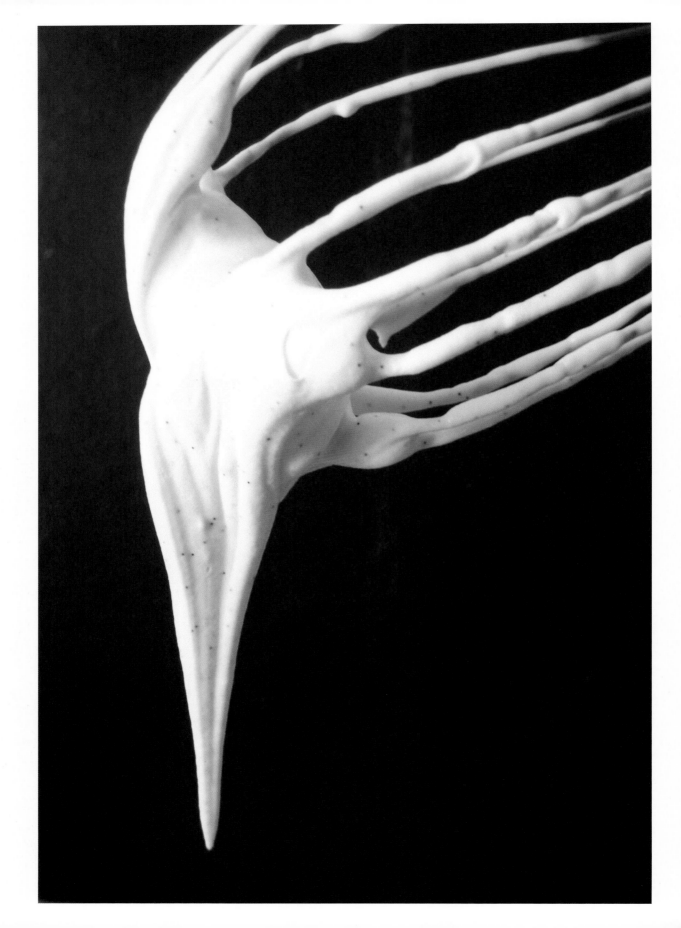

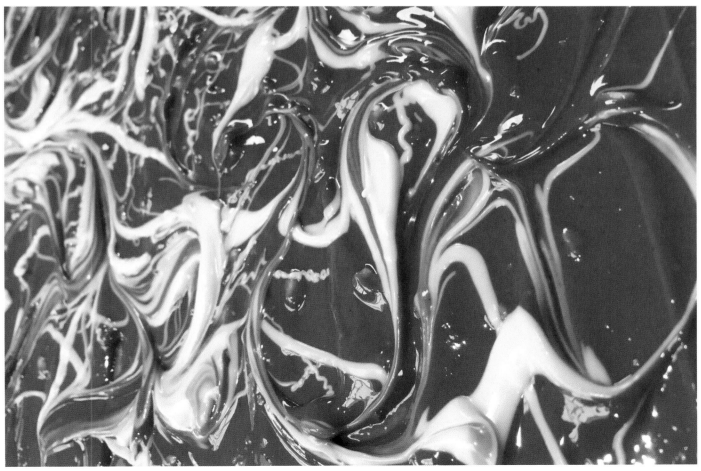

ices

Ice cream is generally made with cream and eggs, making it very rich. It also normally has around 60% air whipped into it and must contain a minimum of 10% butterfat.

Gelato generally contains no eggs, has less fat and only around 20% air whipped into it, making it denser, sweeter and more intense.

Sorbet contains no dairy and is simply a fruit base mixed with a sugar syrup. It is clean, sharp and refreshing.

cacao nib & brown bread gelato

Makes approx. 500ml

175g whole milk
4tbsp cornflour
175g whole milk
350g double cream
75g demerara sugar
1 Madagascan vanilla pod
pinch of salt
50g brown bread
30g cocoa nibs
25g maple syrup

i. Preheat oven to 200°C. Whisk together the cornflower and milk until smooth. Set aside.

ii. Split the vanilla pod, separating the pod and seeds. Bring the milk, cream, sugar, vanilla seeds, vanilla pod and salt to a gentle simmer. You are aiming for around 72°C, but take care not to boil.

iii. Add the cornflower mixture to the warm cream. Whisk thoroughly and cook out for 5-6 minutes, until thickened.

iv. Pass through a fine sieve, discarding the vanilla pod. Cool at room temperature.

v. Meanwhile, tear up the bread and place on a silicone line baking sheet. Bake for 12-15 minutes, until crisp and golden. Remove from oven allow to cool. Blitz to breadcrumbs and put into an airtight jar.

vi. Add the cacao nibs and maple syrup to the cream, cover and place in the fridge to infuse overnight.

vii. The following day add the breadcrumbs and then churn in an ice cream machine or KitchenAid ice cream bowl. Pour into a suitable plastic container and store in freezer until required. Use within 12 months.

chocolate ice cream

Makes approx. 1.2ltr

200g dark chocolate
250g whole milk
250g double cream
25g caster sugar
4 eggs
150g sugar
150g water
100g dark chocolate callets

i.   Heat the milk, cream and sugar to 70°C.

ii. Pour over the chocolate and emulsify until smooth.

iii. Make a simple sugar syrup by dissolving he sugar in water and bring to the boil. Pour the hot syrup over the eggs and whisk.

iv. Add to the chocolate mix and place over a bain marie.

v.   Continue to heat gently until the temperature reaches 70° C continuously stir.

vi. Chill the mixture.

vii. The following day, add the mixture to an ice cream machine or KitchenAid ice cream bowl. Add the chocolate and churn. Pour into a suitable plastic container and store in freezer until required. Use within 12 months.

white chocolate limoncello sorbet

Makes approx. 1ltr.

250g caster sugar
500g water
100g white chocolate
175g rose limoncello
(*see page 39*)

The day before:

i.   Bring the sugar and water to the boil to dissolve the sugar. Meanwhile melt the chocolate.

ii. Allow to cool and add the limoncello and melted chocolate. Chill in the fridge overnight.

The following day:

i.   Blitz in a liquidiser or food processor.

ii. Add the cool mixture to an ice cream machine or KitchenAid ice cream bowl and churn. Pour into a suitable plastic container and store in freezer until required. Use within 12 months.

iii. Let the sorbet soften for 5-10 minutes before serving.

white chocolate & pineau des cherentes sorbet

Makes approx. 1ltr.

For the base:
125g caster sugar
200g water
50g white chocolate
85g Pineau des Charentes

The day before:

i. Bring the sugar and water to the boil to dissolve the sugar. Meanwhile melt the chocolate.

ii. Allow to cool and add the Pineau des Charentes and melted chocolate. Chill in the fridge overnight.

For the Italian Meringue:
50g caster sugar
5g glucose syrup
15g water
25g egg white
a few drops of lemon juice

The following day:

i. Heat the sugar, glucose and water in a copper pan. Heat to 130C. Meanwhile whisk the egg whites and a few drops of lemon juice in a mixing bowl, until soft peaks are formed.

ii. Whilst whisking slowly, pour in the hot syrup. Once all has been added, whisk on fast for 5 minutes until glossy. Set aside and allow to cool.

iii. Blitz the sorbet mixture in a liquidiser or food processor. Add the mixture to an ice cream machine or KitchenAid ice cream bowl.

iv. Remove from the machine and fold in the Italian meringue.

v. Pour into a suitable plastic container and store in freezer until required. Use within 12 months. Let the sorbet soften for 5-10 minutes before serving.

cacao pulp sorbet

Makes approx. 500ml

75g caster sugar
75g water

The day before:

i.   Bring the sugar and water to the boil to dissolve the sugar. Allow to cool and chill in the fridge overnight.

350g cacao pulp
1tbsp lemon juice

The following day:

i.   Mix the syrup with the cacao pulp and lemon juice. Blitz in a liquidiser or food processor.

ii.   Add the cool mixture to an ice cream machine or KitchenAid ice cream bowl. Add the chocolate and churn. Pour into a suitable plastic container and store in freezer until required. Use within 12 months.

iii.   Let the sorbet soften for 5-10 minutes before serving.

savoury

I love sandwiches, but this has to be my favourite ever sandwich! The four key ingredients all have compounds within them that work so well together. Chicken works with salty bacon, which works with piquant blue cheese, which is perfectly balanced with a hit of dark chocolate.

If there is one recipe you have to try, this is it!
You will never look back.

chicken, bacon, blue cheese & chocolate sarnie

Makes 1 sandwich

2 chicken fillets

1tsp olive oil

2 rashers of smoked bacon

2 slices of sourdough

30g of creamy blue cheese

30g savoury chocolate spread
(*see page 149*)

Handful of mixed salad leaves

Preparation:

i. Preheat oven to 180°C.

ii. Heat a cast iron chargrill pan until smoking. Massage the oil on the chicken. Seal for 1 minute on each side. Transfer to a baking tray and finish in the oven for 8-10 minutes, or until cooked through. Season with salt and pepper and allow to rest.

iii. Whilst the chargrill pan is still hot, cook the bacon for 1-2 minutes on each side. Pop onto the baking tray with the chicken to keep warm.

iv. Slice & lightly toast, either in the hot chargrill pan or a toaster.

Build your sandwich:

i. Spread the chocolate spread onto both slices of toast.

ii. Crumble the cheese onto one slice.

iii. Slice the chicken and place on top.

iv. Follow with the bacon and top with salad leaves.

v. Finish with the slice of chocolate covered toast and enjoy!

spiced pulled pork
butternut, psb, white chocolate mash

Serves approx. 10 people (plus leftovers)

Spice Rub:
10g dried thyme

10g dried oregano

5g black peppercorn

30g smoked paprika

70g granulated sugar

30g salt

Pork:
3kg pork shoulder

Garnish:
2kg potatoes

25g white chocolate

50g butter

50g whole milk

1 butternut squash

Drizzle of olive oil

Pinch of chilli flakes

30 stems of PSB
(purple sprouting broccoli)

cacao nib butter
(*see page 150*)

i. Mix all of the dry spices together in a pestle and mortar. Place into a jar and store for up to 6 months.

Prepare the night before:

i. Ask your butcher to prepare the pork shoulder for you for slow cooking. Lay onto a piece of foil and rub with oil. Massage in the spice rub, ensuring that the whole pork shoulder is covered. Cover and allow to rest in the fridge overnight.

The next morning:

i. Heat your Oven or BGE to 100°C. Place the pork shoulder directly onto the shelf or grill with a 3-4cm deep drip tray underneath (to catch all of the delicious juices!). Slow cook for a minimum of 8 hours.

Later that afternoon:

i. Remove the pork from the Oven or GBE, wrap tightly in foil and allow to rest. Turn up the heat to 200°C. The perfect joint will have a dark pink "smoke ring" (see photo opposite).

ii. Peel the potatoes and place into a pan of lightly salted cold water. Bring to the boil and then simmer for approximately 20 minutes, or until the potatoes are cooked through and tender. Drain, remove from heat and add the butter, chocolate and milk. Mash through a moulin for a smooth finish and check the seasoning.

iii. Whilst the potatoes are cooking, peel and slice the butternut squash. Toss in the oil and season with chilli flakes, salt and pepper. Lay a single layer on a baking tray in the Oven or BGE for about 15-20 minutes.

iv. Bring a large pan of salted water to the boil. Blanch the PSB for about 3-4 minutes, until just tender. Drain and set aside.

v. Add a splash of water to the drip tray juices and heat until the desired constancy is reached.

To serve:

i. Shred the pork into large chunks with a fork and mix with the pan juices.

ii. Serve with the roasted squash, cooked PSB, a good dollop of mash and finish with slice of Cacao Nib Butter. Serve any leftovers in a pitta bread with salad!

Top Tip

I like to marinate it before I go to bed. Cook it
the next morning before I go to work and when
I get home its ready to knock up some mash
and enjoy in the sunshine!

BGE (Big Green Egg)

pasta courgetti
chocolate mojito pesto
Makes approx. 2 portions

3 courgettes (green or yellow)

1tbsp olive oil

150g red & yellow baby plum tomatoes

150g fresh pappardelle ribbons

40g chocolate mojito pesto (*see page 151*)

2 tbsp Parmigiano-Reggiano

1 tbsp cacao nibs

Drizzle of unrefined green olive oil

i. Bring a pan of salted water to the boil.

ii. Put a dry wok onto heat. Meanwhile, spiralise or grate the courgettes. Add the oil to the wok and stir fry the courgettes for 3-4 minutes. You may need to drain off any water that comes out of the courgettes.

iii. Add the halved tomatoes. Toss through and gently squeeze. Set aside.

iv. Cook the fresh pasta in the boiling water for 2-3 minutes. Drain and add to the wok. Stir through the pesto.

v. Serve in pasta bowls. Finish with a good shaving of Parmigiano-Reggiano, cacao nobs and a drizzle of olive oil.
Buon appetito!

Top Tip

This is a super speedy supper.

Smaller courgettes work better for this as they contain less water, allowing the frying to 'stir fry' rather than 'poach'.

This is inspired by the classic Sicilian dish, *pesto alla trapanese*. You basically muddle all of your ingredients together, squeezing out all of the incredible flavour, and toss through some fresh pasta. The nibs add texture and really enhance the pesto!

White chocolate is used in this recipe in place of oil when finishing the risotto. The result is an intense creamy risotto, with sweet butternut squash and earthy blue cheese. Finish with cacao nibs to cut through the sweetness.

butternut, blue cheese & cacao risotto

Serves 4

1 small butternut squash

2 white onions

2 garlic clove

300g arborio rice

900ml chicken stock

50g Parmigiano-Reggiano

25g white chocolate

25g strong blue cheese
(my favourite is Remembered Hills)

4 slices cacao nib butter
(see *page 150*) or a handful of nibs

grated dark chocolate, 100%

grated Parmigiano-Reggiano

i.   Preheat the oven to 190°C.

ii. Peel and dice the butternut squash into 3cm pieces. Place on a roasting tray with a tickle of olive oil and season. Roast for about 30 minutes until tender and just golden.

iii. Meanwhile, heat the oil in a heavy based casserole dish. Over a medium heat cook the onion slowly for 10 minutes, until soft and translucent. Add the garlic and rice, stir for 2 minutes.

iv. Add the hot vegetable stock one ladle at a time, occasionally stirring. This will create a creamy texture. Once the liquid has been absorbed, add another ladle until all stock has been used.

v.   Once the risotto is cooked *al dente* (with a slight bite), remove from heat and add the roasted butternut. Grate in the Parmigiano-Reggiano and white chocolate, crumble in the blue cheese, stir and check the seasoning. Put a lid on and allow to rest for 8-10 minutes.

To serve:

i.   Spoon the risotto into a shallow bowl. Place a slice of cacao nib butter in the centre. Finish with more grated Parmigiano-Reggiano and a good grating of chocolate.

A real Friday night treat! Rump steak is full of flavour and so tender if cooked well.

Rich bitter chocolate is a match made in heaven with beef or game, and adds an amazing amount of depth.

ultimate cacao crusted rump steak

chips, tomatoes, mushrooms, chocolate & peppercorn sauce

Serves 2

2 large potatoes
(Maris Piper are best)

1tbsp olive oil

1 beef tomato

2 8oz top-rump steaks

2 tsp raw cocoa powder

2tbsp cacao nibs, crushed

150g wild mushrooms
(Oyster, Shitake, Enokitake,
Eryngii)

1 garlic clove

100g beef stock

50g double cream

30g dark chocolate,
85% Venezuelan

1tsp green peppercorns

twist of black pepper

i.   Preheat oven to 220°C. Peel and slice the potatoes into wedges. Toss in oil, season and lay onto a baking sheet. Roast for approximately 25-30 minutes, until golden and crisp.

ii. Cut the tomato in half, season and halfway through cooking the wedges, add to the tray.

iii. Remove your steak from the fridge about 1 hour before you are ready to cook it. Heat a dry pan until smoking. Add the oil and carefully seal the steak. Turn the steak every 30 seconds - this builds up an even colour, but also ensures that it is cooked through evenly. Cook to your liking - 3-4 minutes for rare, 5-6 minutes for medium, 8-10 minutes for well done. Remove from pan and roll through crushed cacao nibs and powder. Allow to rest for 5-10 minutes.

iv. Whilst the steak is resting, add another 1tsp of oil to the steak pan and the mushrooms. Throw in one bashed garlic clove. Cook and stir for 5 minutes. Remove and set aside.

v.   Whilst the pan is still hot and on full heat, add the beef stock and reduce by half. Add the cream, green peppercorns and freshly cracked black pepper. Bring to the boil, remove from heat and add the chocolate. Stir.

To serve:

i.   Place your steak on a large plate and top with a slice of cacao nib butter. Serve alongside the wedges, mushrooms, tomato and salad leaves. Finish with the chocolate and peppercorn sauce.

Top Tip

I always have a large baking sheet to hand for resting. I place everything on here and keep it in the bottom of the oven or warming drawer until you are ready to serve.
This will make sure everything stay perfectly warm.

best ever burger!

Makes approx. 8

Be warned, when eating this you will get very messy!

The ground up nibs add a real fruity depth to the burger. Layered up between a soft and sweet brioche bun is the perfect way to enjoy this. Burger, bacon and pickles, topped with slaw, a runny egg and tangy chocolate ketchup ... have I missed anything!

1kg minced beef

30g cacao nibs

15g dark chocolate, 90%

salt and pepper

Make the burgers:

i. Grind the nibs in a pestle and mortar to a sandy texture. Add to the mince beef, along with the grated chocolate, salt and pepper. Be very gentle and divide the mixture into 8 rounds. Gently shape but don't press too hard otherwise your burgers will be tough!

1 carrot

1 white onion

½ pointed cabbage

½ bulb fennel

4-6 tbsp mayonnaise

Salt and pepper, to taste

seeded brioche buns

Make the slaw.

i. Using a very sharp knife shred the cabbage, fennel, onion and carrot into paper thin strips (this is the key to a brilliant slaw). Add enough mayonnaise to just combine and season well. Cover and store in the fridge until required.

Fire up the BGE or BBQ:

i. Heat with either a griddle or ceramic plate to about 200°C. Toast your brioche buns whilst warming up and set aside.

ii. Cook your burgers with a lid on for about 5-6 minutes on each side, until cooked through.

8 rashers of smoked streaky bacon

After 5 minutes:

i. Cook the bacon until crispy.

8 eggs

After another 2 minutes:

i. Put the eggs on the ceramic plate or in a pan and cook until the whites are cooked, but the yolks are still runny.

To finish:

i. Top the burgers with the bacon and then the cheese. Cover with a lid to create steam to melt the cheese.

Chocolate ketchup (*see page 150*)

salad leaves

pickles of your choice

To serve:

i. Place your loaded burger onto the base of the brioche bun, top with the egg, salad, slaw and pickles. Place the ketchup on the top have of the brioche bun and top the burger. Enjoy and get messy!

I had the privilege of teaching Bajan students some European recipes when I graduated from university, and in return I tasted some of the finest food the Caribbean has to offer, from flying fish sandwiches to incredible jerk chicken.

As cacao grows in the Caribbean, it seemed a shame not to pair it with the aromatic Bajan spices. For best results, cook slowly on a BBQ and then turn up the heat to get that classic charcoal crisp finish! It's got a real kick, so serve alongside some cooling slaw and traditional 'rice'n'peas'.

Jerkao Chicken
rice 'n' peas, slaw, salad

For the marinade:

1tsp salt

2 garlic cloves

2tsp onion powder

2tsp cacao nibs

1½ tsp ground allspice

1 tsp dark brown sugar

½ tsp ground ginger

½ tsp black pepper

¼ tsp cocoa powder

¼ tsp ground cinnamon or cassia

¼ tsp ground cloves

¼ tsp chilli powder

½ tsp dried thyme

½ tsp dried marjoram

¼ tsp nutmeg or mace

1 whole chicken or 6 breasts or 8 thighs (whichever you prefer)

20g oil

For the slaw:

1 carrot

1 white onion

½ pointed cabbage

½ bulb fennel

4-6 tbsp mayonnaise

salt and pepper, to taste

For the rice 'n' peas:

450g basmati or long grain rice

1 x 400g tin of red kidney beans

large handful of fresh parsley

The day before:

i. Make your marinade by grinding your garlic and salt in a pestle and mortar. Once a paste is formed, add the cacao nibs and grind. Add in all of the remaining marinade ingredients and mix well. Set aside.

ii. If using a whole chicken, prepare as you wish - chasseur style trim, or simply remove the legs, breasts, wings and not forgetting the oysters!

iii. Place the chicken into the marinade and coat every part of the meat, massaging as you go. Cover and store in the fridge overnight. Clean down thoroughly.

The following day:

i. Make your slaw in the morning. Using a very sharp knife shred the cabbage, fennel, onion and carrot into paper thin strip (this is the key to a brilliant slaw). Add enough mayonnaise to just combine and season well. Cover and store in the fridge until required.

ii. Fire up your BBQ or BGE and set to around 150°C Place your chicken on the griddle and cook with the lid on for 1-1½ hours, until the chicken is meltingly tender.

15 minutes before you want to serve:

i. Once tender, turn up the heat to about 220°C and colour the chicken. Once the chicken is quite dark and sticky, remove from the heat and place in a Tupperware dish. Cover and rest until required.

ii. Meanwhile, wash the rice under cold running water. Cook the rice in boiling salted water for 8 minutes. Add the drained kidney beans and continue cooking for a further 5 minutes. Check the rice is al dente and drain. Check seasoning.

To serve:

i. Serve the tender aromatic chicken with a spoonful of rice 'n' peas, slaw and a little salad. You can always shred and serve in a bap if you prefer!

condiments

A condiment is designed to enhance food and comes from the Latin *condimentum*, meaning "spice, seasoning, sauce".

This chapter takes your basic condiments and gives them a powerful chocolate kick. Remember, chocolate is actually a flavour enhancer and seasoning in itself, so if you're like me you will have a salt, pepper and cacao mill on your table!

sweet choco-nut spread

Makes approx. 2 x 250g jars

75g hazelnuts
75g almonds
200g sugar
1tbsp water
50g nibs

For the praline:

i. Preheat the oven to 180°C. Spread the nuts onto a silicone lined baking sheet and toast for 5-10 minutes, until golden.

ii. Meanwhile, make a caramel with the sugar and water, slowly heating to 171°C. Whilst hot, add the warm nuts, nibs and stir. Pour straight onto a silicone lined baking sheet. Allow to cool and set.

iii. Once cool completely, break up and blitz in a mixer to a powder. Store in a tightly sealed sterilised jar for up to 6 months.

200g chocolate
250 cream
175g praline

For the spread:

i. Heat the cream in a heavy based saucepan to 70°C.

ii. Pour the warm cream over the chocolate and stir to melt the chocolate and emulsify. Stir in the praline and pour into sterilised jars.

iii. Cool at room temperature before transferring to the fridge to set. Store in the fridge for up to 3 weeks.

Top Tip

Use praline to make other delights - caramelised nut brittle, baklava, sprinkle into porridge or add to buttercream for cakes!

savoury chocolate spread

Makes approx. 1 x 250g jar

120g dark chocolate
15g balsamic vinegar
95g cream cheese
20g Worcestershire sauce

i. Melt the chocolate to 35°C. Allow to cool slightly.

ii. Beat the balsamic vinegar and Worcestershire sauce into the cream cheese. Once the chocolate is cool, beat in the cream cheese mixture. Season with salt and pepper. Thoroughly mix and pour into a sterilised jar.

iii. Use immediately or store in refrigerator and use within 2 weeks.

chocolate ketchup

Makes approx. 1 x 300g log

18 fresh tomatoes
1 onion, chopped
2 garlic cloves, crushed
1 roasted red pepper, chopped
(from a jar)
20g dark brown sugar
20g date nectar
1 tsp soy sauce
1tsp tamarind paste
25g Modena balsamic vinegar
¼ tsp black pepper
½ tsp smoked paprika
¼ tsp dried chilli
¼ tsp mixed spice
50g chocolate

i. Preheat the oven to 180°C.

ii. Half the tomatoes and lay flat on a baking tray, cut side up. Season with salt and pepper and roast until golden for about 45 minutes.

iii. In a heavy based pan, sauté off the onion and garlic cloves for 4-5 minutes, over a medium heat.

iv. Add the pepper and cook for a further 3-4 minutes. Add the cooked tomatoes and all other ingredients, except for the chocolate.

v. Cook on a low heat for about 30-45 minutes, until thickened.

vi. Use a stick blender to blitz and make smooth. If it is a little thick add a splash of water, if it is too thin cook out for a little longer.

vii. Once the correct consistency (like ketchup) add the chocolate. Stir until mixed in. Check the seasoning and transfer to a

cacao nib butter

Makes approx. 1 x 300g log

250g cultured butter, softened
50g cacao nibs

i. Lightly crush the cacao nibs in a pestle and mortar.

ii. Add the butter and continue bashing until thoroughly mixed.

iii. Place the butter onto a sheets of parchment paper. Form into a log and roll tightly, twisting both ends. Refrigerate overnight and cut off a slice when required.

chocolate mojito pesto

Makes approx. 1 x 250g jar

15g fresh basil
5g fresh mint
Pinch of salt
40g pine nuts
20g cacao, 100%
40g Parmigiano-Reggiano
90g green olive oil
1tsp Mount Gay rum
½ lime (juice only)

i. In a pestle and mortar, bash the basil, mint and salt.

ii. Add the pine nuts and cacao nibs. Slightly crush.

iii. Add the Parmigiano-Reggiano and mix.

iv. Add the olive oil, rum and lime juice. Mix thoroughly and pour into a sterilised jar.

v. Use immediately or store in the fridge for up to 2 weeks.

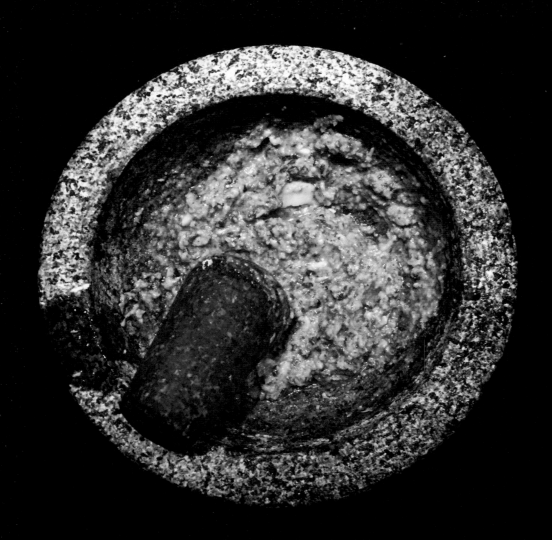

chocolate dressing
Makes approx. 1 x 150g bottle

100g balsamic
50g cacao nibs
10g dark chocolate

100g unrefined green olive oil
50g chocolate vinegar

---

i.   Infuse the balsamic, nibs and chocolate in a glass jar. Leave at ambient temperature for 24 hours. Drain.

ii. For every 50g of infused vinegar, add 100g of oil. Pour into a sterilised jar and emulsify by shaking thoroughly. Use immediately or store at ambient temperature for up to 6 months.

iii. The oil and vinegar will naturally separate, so just shake it up before you use it!

drinks

kuku u kul hot chocolate

Makes approx. 1 cup

For the spiced chocolate:

½tsp coriander seed
¼tsp cumin
1¼ tsp mixed spice
1/8 tsp paprika
1/8 tsp chili powder
1/8 pepper
1/8 tsp salt
1 star anise
1/8 tsp fennel seeds
250g chocolate, 55%
Zest of 1 large orange

To make the spiced chocolate:

i. Grind all of the spices down in a pestle and mortar. They need to be as fine as possible.

ii. Add the ground spices and freshly grated orange zest to the tempered chocolate (*see page 19*). Stir and set on a piece of silicone or in a bar mould. Allow to set for 24 hours. Once et, break up and store in a sealed jar at ambient temperature for up to 12 months.

40g spiced chocolate
120g water

To make the hot chocolate:

i. Heat the water to about 70°C, pour over the broken spiced chocolate. Whisk, pour into a cup and enjoy.

Traditionally hot chocolates were made with water, allowing the flavour of the chocolate to come through. Alternatively replace the water with milk, cream or nut milk for a richer finish.

This is based on the first ever experience of chocolate, where the Meso Americans cracked open the cacao pods, sprinkled in local spices and topped with water. This is basically a spiced hot chocolate, not too sweet and made with water not milk, to bring out the complex clean flavours.

cacao nib & mint tea

Makes approx. 2 cups

Chocolate and mint is a classic combination, as is mint tea. But have you ever tried brewing fresh mint leaves with cacao nibs in a teapot? It is so refreshing, yet complex. Brew for at least 5 minutes to get maximum flavour.

400g water
2 tbsp cacao nibs
sprig of fresh garden mint

---

i.   Heat water to 90°C, just off boiling point.

ii.   Pour over the cacao nibs and fresh mint in teapot or cafetière. Infuse for 5-8 minutes.

iii. Drain and enjoy!

Friday night mocha

Makes approx. 1 cup

For the mocha mix:
230g 73% dark chocolate
140g vanilla sugar
90g Barbados amber sugar
220g instant coffee

To make the mocha mix:

i. You can make this ahead and store in an airtight jar.

ii. Chop the chocolate into small chunks. Mix well in a bowl with the sugars and coffee. Transfer to a jar and use as required.

For the mocha drink:
115g whole milk
3tbsp mocha mix

To make the drink:

i. Place the milk in a saucepan along with three heaped teaspoons of the mocha mix. Heat to just simmering, about 80°C, lightly whisking as you go.

For the vanilla chantilly:
65g double cream
pinch vanilla paste
1tsp icing sugar

ii. Whilst the milk is coming to a simmer, whisk together the cream, vanilla and sugar until soft peaks are formed.

iii. Once warm, pour the mocha into your favourite cup and top with a heaped spoon of whipped Chantilly (and marshmallows if you like!). Enjoy!

cacao masala chai

Makes approx. 1 cup

This is inspired from my travels throughout India. I love how the complex warm spices work in harmony with the malty Indian chocolate. Try a 54% Indian chocolate made with coconut milk.

150g water, milk or coconut milk
1tbsp cacao nibs
20g 54% Indian chocolate
3g Chai Infusion (*see page 37*)

i. Heat liquid to 90°C, just off boiling point.

ii. Pour over the cacao nibs and chocolate. Infuse for 10 minutes. Add the chai infusion, drain and enjoy!

spiced poached pear & cacao nib cooler

Makes 2 servings

1/2 cinnamon stick
1 star anise, crushed
2 cloves
1/4 tsp vanilla seeds
10g cacao nibs
500g pear juice

i. Place all of the spices and cacao nibs in the pear juice. Allow to infuse in the fridge for 16 hours, or overnight.

ii. Drain through muslin cloth and pour into a sterilised bottle. Store in the fridge and use within 3 days.

iii. Serve neat over ice, garnished with a slice of caramelised apple and crushed cacao nibs.

cacao & coconut shake

Makes 2 glasses

Milkshakes are one of my guilty pleasures ...

Coconuts remind me of walking through the streets in Thailand, where they are everywhere! Pairing coconut with a Vietnamese or Caribbean chocolate works brilliantly as they have strong fruity notes and a strong maltiness. Try to find young Thai coconuts as they are incredible aromatic.

20g coconut milk
120g coconut water
80g water
10g coconut sugar
10g date nectar
10g cacao powder

i. Place all of the ingredients into a liquidiser. Blitz until combined.

ii. Pour over a glass of ice, top with a scoop of brown bread gelato (*see page 123*) and enjoy!

Siam cooler

30g cacao nibs
2 lime leaves
1cm piece of galangal
1 stalk of lemongrass
1 lime, zest
1 fresh chilli
10g fresh coriander
5g fresh basil
5g fresh mint
1 sprig lemon thyme
5cm quill of cinnamon
5 green cardamom pods
pinch of turmeric
750ml coconut water

i. Place all of the dry ingredients in a glass bottle or cocktail shaker.

ii. Cover with the coconut water. Seal with a lid and give it a good shake.

iii. Place in the fridge for around 30 minutes. You can leave for as long as you want, but this amount of time allows for the delicate spices to come through, without being too overpowering.

iv. Drain through two pieces of muslin cloth and return to a clean, sterilised bottle. Drink over ice immediately, serving with a twist of lime, a lime leaf, a slice of mango and a sprinkling of cacao nibs of course!

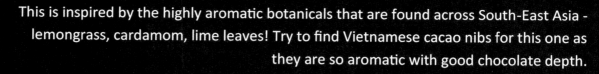

This is inspired by the highly aromatic botanicals that are found across South-East Asia - lemongrass, cardamom, lime leaves! Try to find Vietnamese cacao nibs for this one as they are so aromatic with good chocolate depth.

This is refreshing to drink on its own - or use as an infusion to flavour a cocktail, ganache or truffle.

cold brew rum sour

Serves 1

Inspired by the classic Whiskey Sour,
the infused rum takes this cocktail to the next level.

The smoked oil adds a little depth to the drink
as well as giving a velvety body to the texture.

For the infused rum:
1 bottle Mount Gay Rum
100g cacao nibs
50g coffee (ground)

To make the infused rum:

i. Add the coffee and cacao nibs into your bottle of rum. Leave for a minimum of 2 weeks. Drain and store.

50ml shot infused Cacao & Coffee Rum
25ml shot fresh lime juice
25ml shot sugar syrup
50ml shot aquafaba
1tsp smoked olive oil

To make the cocktail:

i. Add all ingredients to a shaker and shake hard without ice for 1 minute.

ii. Add ice and shake for a further 1 minute.

iii. Pour into a glass and enjoy!

Top Tip

Don't throw the waste away ... use the pressed cacao nibs and coffee in ice cream or on granola!

glossary

Bain-Marie
A water bath or double boiler used to slowly heat, melt or keep items warm.

Big Green Egg (BGE)
A kamado-style ceramic charcoal barbecue cooker, allowing you to grill, bake, roast or smoke.

Botanical
A plant part valued for its medicinal, therapeutic, flavour or scent properties.

Brigadeiro
A traditional Brazilian dessert

Callets
Small chocolate chips or buttons, ideal for melting evenly.

Couverture
Professional quality coating chocolate to give a high gloss finish

Dutch processed
Cocoa that has been treated with an alkalizing agent to modify its colour and give it a milder taste

Ganache
An emulsification of chocolate and a liquid (traditionally cream)

Infusion
The process of extracting compounds through the use of solvents

KitchenAid
A stand mixer with various attachments

Spoonula
A spoon shaped Maryse or spatula, ideal for mixing and spreading.

Tempering (pre-crystallisation)
The process of bringing chocolate to its correct crystalline form, through the use of temperate

CHOCOLATE MOULDS / EQUIPMENT / INGREDIENTS
Keylink
Home Chocolate Factory

SPECIALIST INGREDIENTS
Fine Food Specialist
HB Ingredients
Just Ingredients
MSK
Sosa

CHOCOLATE
Chocolate Trading Co.
Cocoa Loco
Cocoa Runners
The Raw Chocolate Company

SPICES
Local markets
Spice Mountain
Wholefoods

OTHER
Source out specialist seasonal products from local producers and go foraging!

SOME OF MY FAVOURITE CHOCOLATE BRANDS
Armedei
Artisan du Chocolat
Cacaosuyo
Chocolarder
Chocolate Tree
Cocoa Loco
Damson
Doisy & Dam
Duffys
Firertree
Grenada Chocolate Company
Hotel Chocolate
Land
Lauden
Madecasse
Marou
Menakao
Michel Cluizel
NomNom
Original Beans
Patrik Roger
Paul A Young
Pump Street Bakery
Rococco
Seed & Bean
Simón Coll
Summerbird
Tony's Chocolonely
William Curley
Willies Cacao

acknowledgements

I would like to thank …

my best friend, my wife and my chief taster **Tessa** for always being beside me,
supporting my dreams and sharing my passion for food and chocolate.

my beautiful daughter **Florence** for making a choctastic mess with me in the kitchen!

my **family & friends** for supporting me throughout my foodie career.

index

index

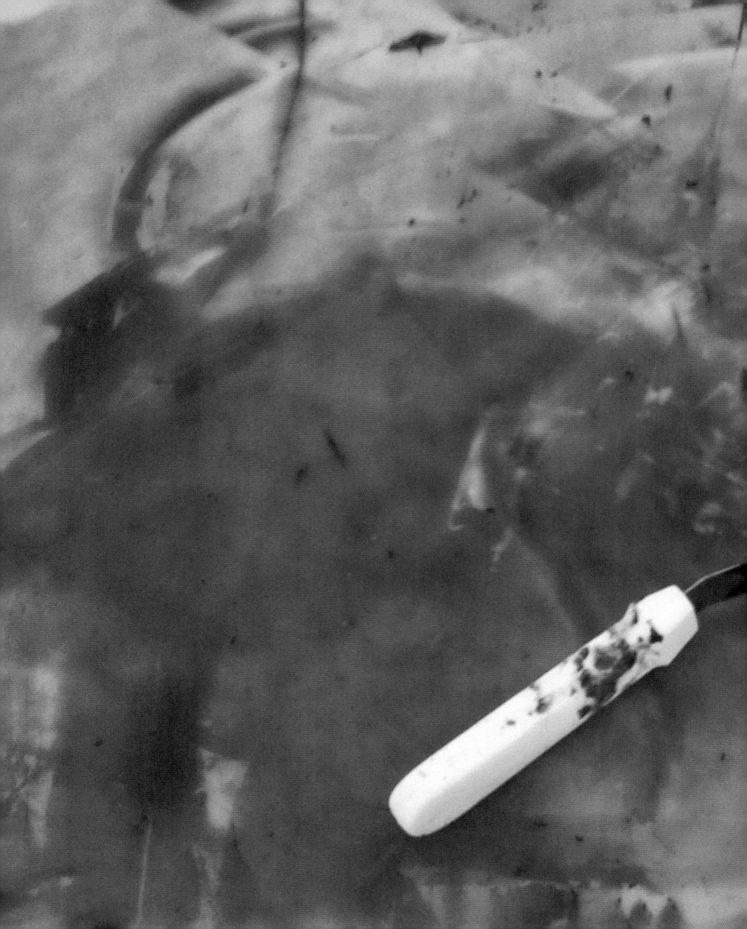

Printed in Poland
by Amazon Fulfillment
Poland Sp. z o.o., Wrocław

62336676R00107